THE PLAYER

How I Traveled the World with an Elite Dating Coach

Part 1

Bostjan Belingar

Foreword by RSD Max

Copyright

The Player: How I Traveled the World With an Elite Dating Coach, Part 1, by Bostjan Belingar

www.bosslifehacks.com

For permissions, general inquiries, or just to say hello, use the email address below:

bostjan.belingar@gmail.com

ISBN: 978-961-283-841-6

Cover Pic by Oliver Mumm: www.tinderboozt.com
Editing by Josiah Davis Book Services:
www.jdbookservices.com
Writing Support by Now Novel:
www.nownovel.com

Disclaimer:

I have tried to recreate events, locales, and conversations from my memories of them. In order to maintain their anonymity in some instances I have altered the names of individuals and places, I may have changed some identifying characteristics and details such as physical properties, occupations, and places of residence.

Table Of Contents

Dedication

This book is dedicated to any guy who has ever battled with the fear of talking to a girl they fancied. It's a long and difficult journey, but it's well worth it. Persist.

For Pirates

Look, I used to pirate a lot. Music, books, films, games, software, you name it.

I'm doing it less now, mainly for two reasons. Number one, there is a lot of free, quality content on the web. Number two, I'm not broke anymore, I have some money, and if a piece of work moves me, or teaches me a valuable lesson, I don't mind paying the price.

So if you are reading this book and didn't buy it, I understand. However, if the book speaks to you, resonates with you, or if it teaches you something, I ask you to do something for me.

If you're broke, drop me a note and let me know you enjoyed it. It means a lot. Share the book or one of my videos on social media, recommend me to someone.

If you do have some money, PayPal (shoot me an email for details) what you think the book is worth to me, or go buy one on Amazon. If you want, drop a note with it too, so I know where it's coming from.

And now enjoy the book. Arrr Arrr!

Foreword

Bostjan? Bostjan's a beast. No wait, actually he's many different things, if I may be honest with you here, dear reader.

He truly is a lot of things. In fact, I haven't seen a guy with that many different depths to his character in a very long time. And trust me, I deal with people all the time. I can read them, see through them, I can tell if they're lying, I know when they're emotional, riled up, excited, or sad.

But with Bostjan it was different. He kept catching me off guard, leaving me surprised. At times, he can be a funny idiot, and minutes later he's wise and philosophical. He can dumb himself down during a fun night out, and he can get his shit together like no one else when it comes to hustling hard.

He can fall asleep ANYWHERE. He can talk to girls at ANY given time. There's no "game switch" he has to hit, he just has that swag all the time. He's got a high sex drive, yet he's always respectful and charming to girls.

So yeah, amongst other things, Bostjan's a beast. And I'm not just saying that. Working with me is hard. When we're under time crunch, I can be incredibly demanding. Almost to the point of obsessive perfectionism during hustle hours, and I don't always find encouraging words for my team members. Bostjan never needed them.

He would just sit down for HOURS and bust out one boring censoring project after another. Meanwhile, he always kept a big smile on his ginger face and occasionally gesticulated to the music he would blast on his earphones.

To be honest, I've always found it quite inspiring watching him work. Most of our work is not fancy, it's not glamorous, it's not... fun. It's hard, monotonous, and quite draining. But Bostjan would always make it fun. He would NEVER stop being happy. Throw this guy into a dull office full of 90-year-olds that have lost their will to live, he would brighten that place up. Throw him into a hospital, people would get cured of cancer.

Bostjan is happy, he really is. Even when he's mad at something or someone, he still looks kind of happy. Even when angry, he's polite. It's weird, but then again, also inspirational. He never seems to get overwhelmed by negative emotions. He's the kind of guy you just CAN'T get mad at.

You know, by the time he joined my team I was a wreck. A total wreck. Me and my assistant, Vini, had been traveling for about a year nonstop. Before that I had ALREADY been traveling for a year. I lost a lot of excitement in my job, my content, and the game in general. When he came on board it was nice and refreshing. This guy would get excited over every seminar we'd do, over every student we'd have. No matter how down a student would feel, Bostjan would compensate for it.

I remember the first month we worked together. We worked for hours during coaching weekends, always on our feet. He'd be shooting infield for six fucking hours straight. I was drained, ready to go home and pass the fuck out, having forgotten who I was or what freaking country we were in. And then Bostjan said:

"Hey, can I stay here at the club and keep approaching?"

"Lol, sure."

I would laugh at him, thinking to myself, *"Watch and learn, bro, you won't be able to keep this up for long."*

Yet, he kept doing it pretty much every freaking weekend. He would wrap up hours of filming, and when everyone was done, he was just getting started. He would join us the next day for breakfast with some crazy story of how he roamed around the empty streets until dawn, getting in the reference experiences, getting in the results.

Maybe it was because he hadn't been traveling for that long, maybe it was because he's younger or, dare I say more naïve. But I believe it's in his personality, in his soul. He would just LOVE the grind, he would just LOVE spreading good vibes... and the girls loved him.

The girls always loved him. He's not a conventionally good looking guy, he's a pale ginger, as short as me (5'7"), he has a weird Slovenian accent, and he smells funny. Haters would say he looks like a very cheap version of the rapper Macklemore. But the interesting thing is that you never FELT that when interacting with him. In over a year of hanging out with him I NEVER heard him complain about his looks, it was simply not part of his reality. And again, girls LOVED him.

I'll never forget looking through his application. I had gotten TONS of applications once it became known that my team was searching for a new travel assistant. Seriously TONS. Bostjan's stood out. Why? Not because of the very personal cover letter, and not because of the valuable video that he had attached to the email. It was because of one little extra reference he had included in the application. Let me copy-paste what he had written:

"I'm attaching a few short (15-20sec) Youtube links so you can connect my voice to my image, hopefully they will make you smile as well, as I know having so many interviews can be tedious."

In the attachment was a vid where he would teach a girl how to breakdance. I had never seen a "pickup artist" interact with a girl like that before. He was funny, charming, VERY nice, and just so polite with the girl. Totally contrary of what a "typical PUA" would potentially do (i.e. negging her, acting higher value, etc.). It seemed like he just had this totally natural connection to the girl. I had to work on this for YEARS, yet he just seemed to have it. Strange, but very impressive.

And seriously, look again at what he wrote:
"...hopefully they will make you smile as well, as I know having so many interviews can be tedious." While every other applicant would write something along the lines of *"give me the job / I want you to be my mentor / I'd do anything/ blablabla"* he was the only one that seemed seriously CONCERNED about my wellbeing. And he was right, going through all those interviews was tedious, and talking to him was refreshing, NOT draining. It was fun, not work.

Guys, I'm seriously randomly typing this off the top of my head. There's so many great things to tell y'all about this guy. When my mom got married again I invited him to the wedding, my entire family loved him. Hell, I'll invite this motherfucker to my own wedding, I'll invite him to my firstborn's birthdays, and I hope we will stay friends forever.

Bostjan's the kind of guy you would always want to have

in your life and I sincerely, from the bottom of my heart, wish him all the wealth and health in this world. If he ran for president I would vote for him; if he built a business, I'd invest in it; if he was getting shot, I would catch that god-damn bullet.

I'll never be as happy as Bostjan, and that's okay, because I know him and that's enough happiness one could ever need. It's too bad he sucks at video games ;)

Now, what are you going to experience through reading this book? Well, pretty much everything.

At some points you might find yourself disgusted, surprised, aroused, emotional. You might disagree with some things and points made (actually, I bet you'll disagree A LOT). You will probably identify yourself with one or the other situation.

The content and stories in this book are dirty, raw, and uncensored. But more than anything else, they're real. There is no better peek behind the curtain of one the most intriguing scenes in today's society; what does it really mean to be amongst the elite, to be touring the world with a full-time dating coach.

Reality might scare you... Enjoy the ride!

RSD Max

Chapter One
MYSTERIOUS APPLICATION

London, August 2015

"We work like fucking animals, I'm talking eighteen-hour work days here. There's barely any time for chasing girls, working on the brand will always have priority. Your main task will be super-gangster, high-pressure, in-club video filming. You will film in some of the world's most prestigious night clubs.

Next, you will be spending a lot of time on video editing. You'll be organizing seminar rooms, working with social media, and even doing stuff like buying groceries and running any other errands."

"Sounds great, I'm excited!"

"You also know, that you have to pay for all of your expenses, right? Each week a different plane ticket, plus all the food and anything else you might need. We'll provide you with free accommodation via our company volunteer network. How much

money do you have?"

"4,000 Pounds, which is 5,000 Euros."

"One thing you have to know is that I will never ask you to do something I haven't done as an assistant myself. I'm saying this because I needed $25,000 for my internship. You don't have enough. What's your backup plan?"

"I've got a good credit score, I can take a loan. Plus, most of our flights are in Europe, you did a lot of USA too."

"Cool. So listen, last question, the obvious one, why do you think you would be a good fit for our team?"

"Max, look. I'm young and full of energy, I want to grab the bull by its balls. I'm not afraid to work hard, I can hustle. This is an amazing opportunity for an adventure, and I love adventures. The fact that I left my home country to create a new home twice can confirm that. Once to Lithuania and once to London, where I reside now."

"Besides that, I'm a very positive person and fun to be around with. I believe my positive energy can be a great addition to a team that's under so much pressure. Also, I'm an experienced traveler and won't complicate things. I learned that during my years of room sharing."

"So look, I'm young, energetic, ready to learn, got money, time, and a shitload of passion. You will not be sorry for taking me!"

"Okay. I'll talk to Vini and then get back to you. Thanks mate!"

"Thank you, bye."

My heart is pounding. I think I did well. I sit in my little box room in East London and go through the interview in my mind one more time. Yeah, I gave it my best. Shit, I was just on a Skype interview with one of the world's best dating coaches. And I think I did well. I go back to sleep, because it's 4am.

I kind of forget the interview in next days, as I'm scheduling a trip to Prague with a good friend. It's actually pretty good to be without a job, I have a lot of time to try new things. For example, trying myself as a Virtual Reality salesman, trying to pitch the new technology to some architectural firms around in London. And dancing for money outside on Trafalgar Square is pretty cool too...

Prague, September 2015

I'm just leaving my hostel and my phone vibrates. I have a new mail. Wait, it's from Maximilian. My heart starts beating really quickly, and I stop in the middle of the sidewalk. I open it and read:

Hey Bostjan!

So Vini and I talked a lot and we decided that we would like to work with you as the new B assistant. If you accept the position it would be awesome if you could join us in Vienna on the 22nd of September for a little test week and if everything goes well you'd continue traveling with us through Europe for the rest of the year, and if possible, even next year.

Let us know!
Max

"WOOOOOOOOOOOOO, OH MY GOOOOOOOD!"

I start screaming and dancing with joy in the middle of

14

Prague. People thought I was weird. I didn't care. My friend is watching me and laughing. I think he's happy for me. I quickly jot down a reply, and triple check it for spelling errors:

Max,

Wohoooo, Yes! I was just screaming with excitement in the middle of Prague, haha :)

I'm definitely in, and will write a more detailed answer when the reality settles in. It's gonna be an amazing journey for all of us!

See you soon,
Bostjan

Chapter Two
MEET BOSTJAN

"Happy Ginger-Hedonist on his Daily Adventures. Featuring Chasing Rainbow Unicorns. Small Dick, Big Heart. Join the Ride :) #idntgvafk"

That's my Tinder description. If you don't know Tinder and you're still living in the Stone Age, you might want to go and Google it.

However, the Tinder description is a bit of a mask. It's kind of true, I am all that. But it's also kind of staged. So let me tell you who I am and why I decided to burn a lot of money, time, and energy in order to follow a dating coach around the world.

Sex.

If I was minimalistic, I'd just write Sex as the reason for my adventures. And a lot of guys (and girls too, mind you) in their 20s would agree. See, we as humans need sex. It's a basic need, according to Maslow.

As my good friend Maximilian would say in one of his

epic speeches while brining back home a beautiful girl off some street or club:

"Everybody loves sex. The bees have sex with flowers. Everyone is thinking about sex all the time. Even the Pope probably jerks off every day".

And my problem was, that I wasn't getting any of it.

Slovenia, Teenage Years

To be honest, my first kiss was pretty magical.

I was 14 and it was after the final primary school dance. I lay in the grass with my girl. I had had a crush on her for years, but never really told her. I managed to get with her that night, because I drank for the first time. No wonder why they call alcohol the social lubricant. So yeah, she was on top of me, we could see the stars, and we were kissing. It's amazing, and very beautiful.

And then she throws up.

She'd been drinking too. Imagine how I felt after. My whole romantic love ideas just got tarnished.

It took two more years for my next kiss. That girl became my girlfriend. It all lasted a grand total of a week or two, and then she got bored of me. I was really sad and quite devastated. My next kiss was at around 18, followed by a relationship. And that was only after I read *"The Game,"* and some other dating advice material.

 # The Game
A book by Neill Strauss, and a concept of the male-female seduction process, the techniques and explanations. You

can have game, or a lack of it. You can do game, you can game with others, you can game girls, or be gamed, or you can be a student of the game.

So why did I suck with girls so much? I can't say. I mean, now, I could tell you why, but I'd have to delve deep into psychotherapy and game theory. But let's not go there now, not yet.

The funny thing was, I was doing well otherwise. I was always likable and far from a social outcast. I had some friends, I was pretty smart, I'd usually know the answer when the teacher asked. I would get picked for the football team as the 3rd choice, which was pretty good.

But girls? Something just didn't click. I would always have fantasies about girls. Girls from school, girls from the street, girls from the books and movies, even video games. I would spend hours thinking about girls, but never doing anything.

A girl from my street? I was "in love" with her for years. I'd dream of different scenarios of how to show my infatuation to her. I'd bring her flowers. I'd fight the class bully for her. I'd invite her to ice-cream. I'd go dancing with her.

I never told her any of that, until much, much later.

Once, I saw a girl I liked at the local disco club, I knew she liked me too. We had known each other for some time, but I never really had the opportunity to do anything about it. So the disco vibe was perfect. We were young, we were both drinking that night. I even remember her looking at me, almost inviting me to come over and do something. Never went up to her, and later on saw another guy kissing her. She became his girlfriend later on. It felt really bad, and I kind of hated myself for being such a coward.

And that would happen again and again and again.

I saw my friends in high-school get together with girls and I just didn't get it. Why not me? I saw them kissing, feeling up each other. I heard stories of how my mates got to touch the girl's boobs. The bravest guy from our class had already had sex at 15. Ah well, I guessed I'd have to settle with porn and vivid fantasies.

At some point I had enough of that. One amazing skill I had, that I still hold and appreciate to this day, was understanding that Google knows everything. I am eternally grateful to my older brother for teaching me this. So I Googled:

"How to get a girlfriend?"

So as most of the guys that get into "pickup," as we call the dating & seduction industry, I found the book called *"The Game"* and it blew my mind. I read some other classics such as *"Double Your Dating,"* and others. And then I started to put it into use.

I met a girl through friends at some birthday party. I started to tease her a little bit, like I had learned from the book. I held eye contact with her. She laughed at my jokes, she liked me. At the end of the night, we all crashed there. I found myself close to her. We hugged and kissed. It felt so amazing, despite having super dry, hangover-dehydrated lips. The next day I felt like the biggest boss ever.

We started to date, which would consist of us meeting and

then hardcore making out for hours at the local bar. I was 18 at the time. After about three months of that, we started having sex. First time was terrible. Put two virgins together and tell them to have sex and you're in for a laugh.

The whole thing lasted for about a year, and it was amazing. I really liked that girl, and I spent some amazing times with her. And for many years after, she'd remain the only girl I had ever introduced to my parents. We cuddled, we started to visit each other, and most importantly, we did what young people in relationships do. We had a lot of sex.

Then I went to uni. I started to meet more and more girls there, I had more and more success. I'd sit close to a cute girl, because why not. I'd flirt when the class group went out together. I'd invite girls out. It was still a kind of hit-and-miss, but at least I had some results.

But this was no coincidence. I would read a lot, I would watch videos on Youtube, and would try to extract the knowledge of the pros. In a few years I swallowed almost all the dating material that could be found online. Hours, upon hours, upon hours. This whole game thing blew my mind!

And I met a lot of cool girls in those years, especially during my ten-month study exchange in Lithuania. That was absolutely crazy. If you're a student, please go on a study exchange. Even if you suck with girls, you will probably still get laid.

However, despite getting some early success, I fucked it up with a lot of girls I met too. It would start of great, but then I'd often times say something too retarded, try to randomly kiss them out of the blue, or something equally stupid. It was a shame, because some of those girls were really cool, and I really liked them. And they were super hot too.

So for about five years, ever since I discovered the game, I would be "gaming" or "pimping,", as we call it, regularly. It means I would walk up to a random girl at a club or on the street, and try to start a conversation. Sometimes it worked, and sometimes it didn't. And I would continue to work on my craft, analyzing it, reading books, and watching videos.

Pimping
Pimping (it) – a slang term which means going out and talking to women which you didn't know before. Another term for it is "cold approach pickup", or just gaming. Usually used by guys in the seduction community.

London, Summer of 2015

I was pretty good at the game then. I was getting laid every now and then, I talked to some of the girls I liked. I didn't really have any longer relationships as I was looking for high-quality girls. The few who I'd met that I would consider getting into a relationship with were somehow not available, or not interested.

I was getting attracted to the game more and more. My job and side hobbies were having less and less importance. The world of seduction was becoming increasingly lucrative, and I was putting more and more emphasis on it. My thought pattern was *"If I can just get this part of my life handled..."*

Later on I realized it doesn't work quite like that.

Anyway, I was in London, and super interested in the game. Recently out of work, but with decent savings in my account. I was thinking of moving to Thailand for a few months to game every day.

And then my buddy hit me up with the info that this guy RSD Max was searching for an assistant to travel the world with him.

I knew who RSD Max was from the online videos I watched. He was the fastest growing dating coach around and a part of the biggest company in the field – Real Social Dynamics.

I was always up for crazy ideas, so I applied. Let me correct myself. I didn't just apply, I seriously kicked ass. I paid a guy to shoot a professional video of me, and sent it as a Video CV instead of the normal boring email.

Guess who got picked.

Chapter Three
LET'S GO ON AN
ADVENTURE

London, September 2015

It's all a haze now. I came back from my vacation in Prague and had about two more weeks in London before embarking on this crazy, life-changing adventure.

I remember I had a weird, slightly melancholic feeling. This seems to always happen when you are about to do something awesome. You kind of know it's gonna be awesome, but you don't know what exactly to expect. Fear starts to creep in through every little crevice in your mind. The old familiarity which you used to hate becomes strangely alluring and... safe.

I was making final arrangements. Renting out my room to a friend, getting all my papers ready, booking the first few weeks of my flights. I didn't really have any girlfriends at that moment, so I was still trying to meet some girls and get laid just before I left.

I Skype called all the people I knew who had any affiliation with RSD and asked all kinds of questions in order to prepare myself to get the most out of the experience.

The last few days before I left, I was hanging out with my friends from London a lot. On my last evening, I made pancakes and we had a few beers as well. Me and five other dudes, probably my closest bunch at the time in London. Nothing special, but enough to give me encouragement and make me feel that I belong somewhere. It confirmed, for the second time in my life, that I could build my whole social circle from scratch, even in a foreign country. It's a very liberating feeling.

The last night in my little box room was the worst and doubts started to howl at me. Regardless, I packed my bags. Actually, I packed my bag. I had only one big blue suitcase and a small backpack. Shit, that's all I own. Those will be my only worldly possessions for some time.

Ah well, fuck it.

I woke up and got the last papers done. I said goodbye to my flatmates, and met with my boss to settle the details of the remote work I would be doing for him during my travels. And then I started to roll with my big blue suitcase towards the airport, which would become a very familiar sight and feeling.

The funny thing of that morning was, all the fear was gone. Big grin on my face, bright sparks in my eyes, full of energy and excitement.

Vienna, here I come.

Chapter Four
MEET MAXIMILIAN

Vienna, September 2015

Tuesday

"Hey Max, I'm in Vienna. Where and when do you want to meet?"

"Hey man, meet me in Starbucks on Maria Hilfer Strasse at 2pm, I'll attach the Google Maps location. Also, bring your laptop. See you soon."

I'm slightly sleep deprived because of a wild night (I'll explain soon), but super excited. It's sunny in Vienna and I hopped on a metro towards Maria Hilfer Strasse.

I love Austrian public transport, nobody gives a damn if you pay or not. You just board the train, and then get off. I heard they have people who control that, but I never experienced it myself, so I wouldn't be bothered to buy a ticket.

It's true that I had 5000€ in my account, but that needed to last for three to six months. Buying a plane ticket every week in addition to club entrances, other transportation and food would be costly. So I needed to be in a money-saving mode. I felt slightly guilty, so I'd promise to myself I'd pay for all my tickets when I'm rich.

Anyway, I find the Starbucks and go in. I look around for a bit and then I see a bearded guy with glasses.

It's Max.

He's of similar size to me, which is pretty short for a guy. He seems quite like a regular dude too, cool. We introduce ourselves, and sit down, both with our laptops out. A sight that would become very, very familiar over the next half a year or so.

We chat for a bit, but we're both not fully relaxed. However, we're both socially calibrated so we don't make a big deal out of it. Instead, he gives me a few initial tasks, like setting up an Evernote (an application to manage projects) account and scheduling a few errands.

Then, a weird incident happens. A tall dude enters and goes straight to Max and greets him in German. I don't understand everything, but I see that Max is confused. After a few minutes of awkward conversation and silence the guy leaves.

"I don't even know that guy, man. He came inside, I don't know how he knew I was here, and just started to talk to me. And then he started to ask me for dating advice. Like I don't have anything better to do all day than wait for people to come and ask me shit. What the fuck. And this sorts of things happen regularly now, like almost every day somebody recognizes me. Most of the people are cool, but some are super weird."

"*Oh, boy,*" I think to myself and continue to work. My computer doesn't work properly. I try to install the video editing software (Adobe Premier), but it's running super slowly. Damn. I was afraid of that - I had an old computer.

We work for another hour or so, then Max tells me that the real work starts tomorrow, once the other assistant, a Brazilian guy named Vini, comes.

However, if I wanted, I could meet Max in the evening and we'll go out and pimp it. Nothing flashy, nothing work-related, just fucking around and pimping. Obviously I'm super down.

I go towards my home and eat in some cheap sushi place. I order everything in German. My German is actually not bad and since we were in Vienna, I'd try to speak German. That came handy in Berlin too, but otherwise I'd stick to English during most of the travels.

When English doesn't suffice, there is always the old-fashioned hand-pointing and weird noise-making. For example, if you are not sure if it's beef, you can simply point to the meat and ask:

"*Moo?*"

Vienna, Later that Evening

I meet Max around 10pm, he has a friend or two joining and my host is with me too. We go to some club and he pays the entrance fee for me. I start to protest, but it's cool, but he insists.

"*I pay club entrances for my assistants. Most other instructors don't do that, but I do. Don't worry, it's cool."*

I get a big grin on my face, thank him, and enter. It's not very busy yet, so we chill and bullshit a bit. He seems pretty cocky. Black pants, slicked-back haircut, a Hawaiian shirt, and an unlit cigarette in his mouth. An almost bored expression on the face, and a strange spark in his eyes.

I open some girls and bring some of them to say *"Hi"* to him. That's good wingmanship code, by the way.

#**Wingman**
Your friend who helps you get the girl. Either by just hanging out with you and thus putting you in an awesome mood, or by actually talking to the girl's friends etc, allowing you to focus on the girl.

#**Open**
The act of starting the interaction with an unknown person. Either verbal by saying "Hi!" or something similar, or nonverbally, for example through eye-contact, gestures, or touch.

If you want good wings to like you and go out with you, introduce hot girls to them. For example, tap a hot girl on the shoulder, smile, and show her to your wing:

"Hey, this is Jake, he's an awesome dude, you should meet him."

And then leave. Done properly, it works like a charm.

Anyway, Max chats with some of the girls I bring in and dismisses others. I see he is evaluating my game, and I am doing the same with his. All the guys in our group had some game, but I could clearly see his one was the best. I was better than most other guys with us too, but nowhere near him.

There was a certain relaxation in him, a clear intent that was beaming out of his eyes. He was not all over the place, yet girls still seemed to notice him and were drawn to him. Good, finally somebody I can learn some things from.

Hours are passing and we are pimping it. I have a lot of fun and am very active, but nothing really flashy happens. This is the beauty and pain of the game. Some nights are crazy, like the one I had the night before. Girls are all over you, you do crazy shit. Other nights, you get rejected a lot, nothing seems to work quite like it should.

At some point I noticed that Max felt completely at home. He was owning the club environment. Knowing which spot is the best, knowing how to talk to the staff, knowing how to act around women. He was completely genuine, blasting out nerdy jokes and girls were loving him for it. He didn't have to try hard to be cool, he just simply fully let go.

I open some hot redhead. She instantly comes closer and gives me the Bambi eyes. I sense she's totally horny and down for some action tonight. As a good wingman, I introduce her to Max and he captivates her instantly.

Bambi Eyes
When a girl's pupils are very dilated, looking straight into your eyes, almost without blinking. You can kind of feel the energy and the "chemistry" as some people would say.

After a minute or so, he gently pulls her a few steps to the right, so he could lean on the wall and have her standing in front of him, talking to him. I see how she's giggling, and how he's holding very strong eye contact with her, she's practically melting.

I go on, feeling good about what I did. Later on, I become a bit desperate, because I wanted to get with a girl that night too. What burns even more is seeing Max still talking to the redhead. I knew that girl was a potential catch. They are at the bar now, having drinks. They are leaning in close to each other, and seem to be in deep conversation.

Ah well, fuck it.

Friendship and being held in good regard is worth much, much more than a random girl. I try to join his set to talk to the friend of his girl, try to wing for him. However, her friend doesn't seem to like me, so Max signals me that he doesn't need help.

Set
A group of people around the girl you want to talk to. It could be only 2 people, the girl and a friend, or it can be a big group.

Another hour later, I see Max talking to the same girl and her friend. They are in the coat check area now. It seems like Max and her are making plans to leave together. What blows my mind at this point is that the friend of the girl kisses her goodbye and goes back to the party. Max and his girl grab their jackets and leave the club.

Usually, the friends try to convince the girl to stay in club. They have to really trust her and be certain that the guy is cool enough to "allow" her leave with him.

I stay in the club, I keep persisting. I have a few good sets, but nothing amazing. My mindset just wasn't the best, I was too tired and too desperate. I decided to leave around

4, get a Viennese snack - *"Sandwich Sammeln."* A sandwich with a Viennese steak inside. That made me happy. Good food always makes me happy.

On my way home I receive a picture. It's from Max. And on the picture is the naked redhead, lying face down on her stomach. I can see her beautiful body and tight ass. Following the picture are two smiley faces. Damn, she's super hot. I reply with a:

"Hahahah, glad you're enjoying yourself, see you tomorrow."

I learned later on that Max is always happier when he gets laid.

I guess that comes with being a dude.

Chapter Five
SPERM ON MY SHOES

Wednesday

Before work the next day, I asked Max a few questions regarding a few of the interactions of the previous night. How did he get the girl's friend to leave? What did he say so the girl just came with him? How did he take a picture of her later on? We talk a little bit, and the topic of the night before meeting him comes up, my first night in Vienna. Remember when I said I had gone without sleep? Well, I went out with my host and ended up at some girl's place.

I tell Max about the interaction. He gets a big grin on his face.

"Well done, bro, that's fucking awesome! Why didn't you say you already got laid, haha. You should totally write up a lay report. You'll motivate and teach other people, and you might even learn something yourself. I used to write a lot of them

myself. Just write it up, and post that shit in the Vienna Inner Circle Facebook group. That's how you'll give some value back to the community."

I wasn't exactly sure of how to write that, but this was my attempt:

Inner Circle
A dedicated Facebook group where players meet and discuss different topics. It's a place to find new wingmen, it's a place to ask questions, and a place to share ideas and resources. Amazing places, that help the community grow.

Player
A guy (or a girl) who games.

Lay Report, September 2015

Vienna Inner Circle Facebook Group

So I land in Vienna on Monday at 10pm, my host is already a bit pissed because I'm late. But I'm very chill. Actually, fucking excited would be a better term - new stage in my life, new journey, new city, a lot of things to be learned and discovered.

Oh, on a funny note, at the airport I already chatted up this cute chick, we talked for like 20min and when I took her number it appeared that I already had it – I think from a street approach that happened a few months ago in London! That was super funny.

#Approach
Same as #Open.

Anyway, at the airport, I use my solid German language skills and get a cool old dude to help me buy the train ticket to the centre. Then I meet my buddy, my host. He takes me to some student dive bar in the centre, which was already busy. Lots of drunk people, loud music, pretty girls. I feel like I'm home.

There we meet a few other players as well - it's really easy to notice them. High-energy guys running around doing crazy things around girls, trying to get their attention. Anyway, my buddy is already talking to a group of girls, so I go around as well. I open a few girls who are super friendly, I like Vienna already. Seems like in all cities, except for London, the girls are super nice haha.

One girl returns my eye contact so I know it's on. I kiss her neck after a few minutes of playful conversation, then I lead her away from the bar:

"Come check out that bridge, it's really cool!"

We go there, and on the way she starts to say something about a boyfriend.

However, she's looking at me with lustful eyes and has no problem being very near to me. I kiss her neck again. She likes it. I tell her to kiss my neck, and she does so willingly. Then I want to make out with her, but she refuses. I try again after some time, she refuses again. No worries, I bring her back to her friends.

Then I go to the dance floor and do some game there. I open like four or five more groups of girls. They like me, but no crazy hooks.

#Hook
Hook is a term for a point where a girl is more inclined to stay and talk to you than to leave. She's comfortable being around you for the time, and from there on you can build up on your interaction.

I stay in one set where I really liked the girl, but it doesn't go anywhere. Then one other chick hooks as well. We talk, she is more laid-back, then she goes to the toilet and tells me to wait for her. We've just talked for five minutes, so I don't wait, I move on. The oldest trick in girl's game. I don't want to be like a dog who waits for her, because that would kill any attraction she had for me.

It's about 1am now. I see two girls at the bar and open them:

"Wohooo, you know how to partyyyy!"

It's a classic high-energy opener. They high-five me back and return the massive "wohoo." Both girls are pretty cute, but far from stunners.

One is a super petite blonde, not very tall, hot body. She's your typical, partying school girl, and she also looks pretty drunk. The other is brunette, a bit taller, with big breasts and a kinky smile. She seems pretty much sober and bored as fuck. The blonde turns to some other dude and the brunette hooks with me.Then I basically game her for like an hour before I get anywhere.

We talk about all kinds of things. I'm cocky-funny, I tease her.

#Cocky-Funny
A slang term coined by David D, suggesting a guy be a combination of a funny guy and a dick when he talks to a girl to make her attracted to him. A cocky-funny guy.

She plays hard to get. I try to hug her, she pulls back a bit. But as time passes, our interaction progresses slightly. I am kissing her neck now, first slowly, then a bit more passionately, and she loves it. Kissing the neck is one of my favorite things, by the way. I like the feeling when the girl starts to breathe heavily after I kiss her neck, and I like it when a girl kisses my neck, it's pretty much like heaven.

However, she won't kiss me no matter what. Back then, I thought I had to always kiss before taking it to the next level. From our conversation, I could feel she's into black humor and kinky sex. So I think of a great idea. I come up with a fantasy role play, I'll be the brother, she'll be my step-sister. So just for the hell of it, I randomly make up a brother and step-sister incest story.

"Yeah, my little step-sister, so what do you think daddy will say when he finds us in the bed together, when he sees you touching my naked chest, my hands all over you, touching you passionately…"

That's when I see she's super into that sort of stuff, and we both get turned on. I see her giving me intense Bambi eyes, I'm guessing she's probably getting wet already. At this point the whole dynamic shifts; I play a little hard to get now, so she has to work a bit for me. For example, when she forgets my name I completely ignore her till she starts physically poking me and apologizes.

In the meantime, some guys come and try to steal her away from me. I mostly let them talk to her because they suck. I can see it. Bad body language, apologetic, approval-seeking and drunk. All major errors when a guy tries to chat up a girl. At some point, I see a potentially dangerous dude coming in. I whisper in her ear that I like her, but if she's not going to pay attention to me I'll pick up some other girl.

And I demonstrated that a few times too. While guys chatted her up and she was flirting with them, I talked to other girls and had them all over me. She saw that, and she realized I was a player. So then when guys came to her and chatted to her she still kind of responded to them, but was coming closer and closer back to me, eventually talking to the guys whilst simultaneously rubbing her ass on my pelvis.

At some point we were at the bar together, and there was a moment when we were just looking into each other's eyes. It seemed like it lasted forever. That was a green light. I put my hand on the back of her head, and gently pulled her in for the kiss. I kissed her a bit, but stopped it soon. I could feel her wanting more.

I could see she was going crazy, that probably never happened to her before. A guy refusing to kiss her when she obviously wanted it. I suggested getting food, which can often times result in you and the girl ending up in the same bedroom. She said we could listen to music later on at her place. Sweet. I knew that she knew, that I know, you know?

By this time she was for sure all wet and ready to be taken home, but we had to take care of her drunk friend too, the blonde. She wouldn't leave her, damn. We tried to get her to come with us, but she didn't want to. She was having too much fun being hit on and having all the dudes buy her drinks. I figured this might take some time, it was 2.30am already.

I needed my coat, because it was in the club next door, so I took my girl with me. Then we go search for an ATM, because I needed some cash – I figured I'll probably need to get a cab later. Meanwhile I do more fantasy role play.

At some corner, when I feel her squeezing my hand hard, I push her to the wall and make out with her. We kiss passionately and our hands are all over each other. I'm super horny, and so is she. I take her hand and put it on my dick which is really hard at the time. She starts rubbing me over the pants, I do the same to her pussy, she starts moaning hard. I take her hand and put it inside of my pants. Then I unbuckle them, to make some space and let her start touching my dick inside my pants.

"Wait, we can't do this here," she says as she's jerking me off with a big, dirty smile on her face. Obviously she's living out her fantasy. Her eyes are burning with fire, as we're standing at some random street corner not caring about the cold and burning with passion.

"Don't worry, baby, just keep going, it feels so good."

"Wouldn't you rather do it in a bed?"

"Yeah, we'll do that too, this is just foreplay."

She was good, and it was really sexy for me too. Mind you, this was not usual for me. I had things like that happen before, but quite rarely, and to be honest it was always a lot of luck too. Usually when it happened, the girl was super down right from the start.

I was really horny and she was great at jerking. I come quickly, and as I turn to the side as I'm ejaculating, some semen finds its way on my green Pumas. Damn, I really liked those. We both laugh about that. Then we kiss a bit more, we realize that a few cars passed us while we were not paying attention, and decide to go back to the club to find her friend.

We get back to the club, I meet some guy and compliment his cap. And him being an awesome and happy drunk bro, he gives the cap to me. What a cool dude, I cannot believe it. I take a picture with him, crack some jokes, then just chill with my girl and have some more guys try to steal her off.

She was super hooked though, so they had no chance. I knew it was time to pull, but her friend wouldn't leave. So at 4am, the club closes, and finally we take off. Again, her blonde friend is chatting with everyone, plus I'm not sure where they live.

I knew I had to act fast now, otherwise some bullshit will happen. Sometimes a drunk dude wants to fight. Sometimes the girls want to go to yet another afterparty. Sometimes they eat too much junk food and get sleepy. This is the time for action.

Fuck it.

"Come girls, I'll get us a cab."

Cab comes, I tell the girls to get in, I jump in the front seat, and tell the driver their address. It was only 15€, and an amazing drive too. The girls were making out in the back and me and the driver were laughing. And it was good ego boost too, because I could see how much the driver admired me.

Anyway, my girl wanted a threesome, I was obviously super down. But the other girl was a bit shy. My gal tried hard to convince her, but in the end it was just my girl and I in her room.

We are kissing, I throw her on the bed. We're not losing any time. As we're kissing I take off my shirt, and soon after I take off hers too. Damn, she had such amazing tits. I kissed all over her breasts and neck and then took of her bra. The feeling when 2 bodies are touching each other, the intense warmth, the closeness, that gets me really horny.

Meanwhile, I continue with the brother and step-sister story, and she's loving it. I feel kind of funny saying these things, but she seems to enjoy it a lot, so I turn it up a notch.

"Oh, yeah, little sister, how does it feel when you're about to fuck your own step-brother? Does it turn you on? Do you feel guilty, you dirty little girl..."

Her eyes were big and round, she was breathing heavy and told me she really wanted me to fuck her right then, she couldn't wait anymore. I take off my boxers, she is also fully naked now. And because I don't know why, I went down on her, even though it's not the most hygienic thing to do after a night out.

I alternated between fingering her and licking her pussy, it was incredibly sexy.

She was super wet and moaning really hard, her hips were rocking back and forth, she and I couldn't wait to have sex. Then just as I am putting a condom on, the bane of all men happens. I have a limp dick.

FUCK!

Seriously, why now!? And as I stress about it, it gets even limper. That happened a lot to me before. I'd often experience this issue when I was with a new girl. The fact that it was like 5am and I was tired as fuck - since I had flown in from London that day - didn't help either.

I could see she was disappointed. She expected some hardcore banging and instead got a limp dick guy. However, she was cool, she tried not to show it, and gave me a really nice blowjob. After some time, I manage to relax and get my dick hard again and we can finally get to business. However, I come pretty fast, and we're both tired so we go to bed.

I finally fall sleep at 7am. I wake up at 10 am, and then it's sex time again. As soon as I wake up I feel an intense boner. I wake her up by kissing her and massaging her pussy. She starts moaning pretty quickly. This time we have intense sex. We're not making love, we fuck hardcore.

She enjoys it a lot apparently, as she screams very loudly. I don't mind, because it's her place anyway. In addition, I like it when a girl is loud, it turns me on and makes me fuck even harder. We change positions several times, and as I'm stimulating her G-spot she comes too. Then we lie in the bed for a bit, we don't really cuddle, which is a shame, because I normally really like that.

She makes some tea, I chat with her for a bit, and then also with her friend who comes around too – they are flatmates. I leave her place shortly after, as I was about to meet with Max soon and I needed to grab my computer.

Before saying goodbye, I asked if she wants to exchange numbers. She gives me a number that I can't find on WhatsApp. I ask for her Facebook, and she writes the name, but can't find it herself. I say that if she writes her email, Facebook will find her for sure.

She doesn't know her email.

I'm not pushy, I figured it was only a one-night stand for her, and she apparently had no plans to see me again. And that's cool with me. I hug her goodbye and walk into the sun with a big grin on my face.

It was almost like a sign from above. I was following my dreams and got blessed for going all in with this crazy world tour travel. I was young and crazy, I had no idea of the scope of experiences waiting for me.

Chapter Six
MEET VINICIUS

Thursday

"Yo, Bostjan, go pick up Vini from the train station and help him get his stuff here."

So I was on my way to meet the third and final member of our team. The team which would, in the next few months, become a team of very close friends and hustlers. So close, we'd learn literally everything about one another. So close, we'd actually start cracking gay jokes. Oops.

I come to McDonalds at the central train station in Vienna. There are a lot of people, but I spot Vini instantly. There's one thing about RSD guys, you can spot them. I can't really tell you what it is. Sometimes they look a little nerdy. Sometimes they look super jacked and in shape. Sometimes you see them checking out girls. There's a lot of different things, but that core similarity can be noticed. I guess it takes one to know one.

Vini's a tall dude. Tall, slim, and rocking glasses. And at the time, a long, single braid, just like the one Obi-Wan had in Star Wars. When I met him he was low in energy and a bit quiet. He said he's got a massive jet-lag, there's a big time difference between Brazil and Europe.

We walk towards Max's Airbnb and chat on the way. He tells me about the flight, how long he's been with Max and some other things. But mainly, I don't torture him with the whole Game Fanboy thing. Like wanting to know how good he is or how good he think Max is, or what his favorite type of girls was, or how many girls he's slept with. Mostly we just chat about random shit.

Game Fanboy
A dude who watches way too many game videos and who's read way too many books on the topic. Someone who thinks that RSD instructors are basically Gods who eat pussy for breakfast. I used to be one.

When we come to Max's Airbnb, Vini crashes on the sofa and falls asleep within a minute. Wow, he really was tired.

A peculiar thing that I noticed about him on the first day was his sneakers. He had the Mizuno running sneakers, a bright orange color. I thought to myself that was a bit funny. How could someone who knows game, someone supposedly good with girls, wear shoes like that? There's zero style to them, except if you're a runner. Later on, I understood. They were comfortable and great for walking. And you walk a LOT when you are an assistant.

In the next days, as he got his strength back, I got to know him a little bit better. He was quite tech-savvy, or a little nerdy if you want. He had amazing game and he was really funny too. Very sarcastically funny, but never in a mean way. I later learned that this sort of cynical humor is what keeps you alive through an ordeal like our world tour. If you can't laugh at how fucked up you are, you quit.

If Max was the mentor/boss figure, Vini was the older brother/friend. He taught me a lot of things. Most importantly, how to operate a $5,000 camera and how to edit the videos. We would buy cheap food together, because none of us were getting paid yet. We would go pimp together on our rare nights off. We'd roll our eyes together when Max was pushing too hard, or had one of his little "perfectionist fits."

He'd give me advice on girls and listen to me when I had a problem. I'd do the same for him. Soon, a strong friendship emerged. This was pure friendship and bromanship. It was different with Max; Max was our bro, but at the same time our boss, which made things a little more complicated. Vinicius, as was his full name, was my bro.

In the next few months we'd travel to more than 20 countries, share everything from laughs and tears to sweat. We'd pick up girls, we'd share joy, frustration, and exhaustion. And much, much more.

Chapter Seven
MY FIRST FILMING NIGHT

Vienna, Friday Night

"Always go through the checklist, man. This is super, super important. If you forget something, you're fucked. Max will get pissed with you and you'll need to go back and get the stuff. Then it's harder to get in the club, you waste more time, more money."

He said that in a super serious voice. It reminded me of master Yoda from Star Wars. I giggled deep inside. Vini sends me the list on my phone. I guess it has happened before and it wasn't nice.

Infield Checklist

-Camera with 16-35mm lens,
-Metabones adaptor
-Both camera caps
-Headphones

-Microphone + cable
-Receiver + cable
-Extra AA batteries
-Extra camera batteries (at least four)
-Extra SD card
-Cash for club cover fee
-Remind Max about silver tape & earplugs

"Ok, Vini, I got everything, thanks."

"Sweet, now we need to practice the story. Cameras aren't allowed in most nightclubs, so you need to know what to say and how to act when the bouncers ask you. Now, the most important thing is that you remain calm at all times. Don't freak out and you're gonna be all good.

Best scenario is that you just walk into the club with all the gear in your pockets. The camera disassembles nicely. As as long as you have big pockets, you're good to go. If they don't pat you down you get in with no problems. Just be chill, normal, look them in the eye, greet them, and walk in. If you're chill, this will be 90% of the time.

When they do pat you down, or spot the camera and tell you that you are not allowed to bring it inside, this is your story:

"Oh, yeah, I know. I was just taking pictures before and didn't want to leave the camera in the car - it's pretty expensive you know, and I had some really bad experiences with that in the past."

Again, remain calm, and look them in the eye when you tell the story. Also, say it in a dismissive way, kind of like you think it isn't a big deal. This will work for the next 9% of the time.

If they're being really hardcore about it, tell them you will leave it in the coatroom for sure. If even that doesn't work, you will try to smuggle it in. For example, you can try tossing it to me over the club fence. If even that is not possible because of the circumstances, we don't want to break the camera, right, you can bring it back home and then return to the club without it. However, if you play it right, this shouldn't happen."

Then he explains a lot to me about exposure, focus, and all the buttons that I will need to use. There were a LOT of different settings to think about. The fact that I had never used a professional DSLR camera before didn't help either.

"Also, play around with the camera settings now. You want to be able to change most of the settings you will need in pitch black, or even without looking. People or staff might spot you in the club if you keep looking at the display.

Your display will be turned off most of the time. Make sure you know how to take out the SD card and switch the batteries without looking too. If it happens, and let's hope it won't, that you get caught, you'll want to remove and hide the SD card before they see the footage. This way you can claim you weren't filming anything and we don't lose the footage. Got it?"

"I think so."

Then Vini, Max and I get going. We walk to the same club from where I pulled from the first night, and I learn it's a club famous for drunk students. Oh, well. This would be my training night. My pants were almost falling down because I had so much weight from the gear in my pockets. I was starting to get seriously nervous.

#Pulling
Going home or to another private location with the girl, from the venue you are at currently.

You see, the camera, once assembled, is a big piece of equipment. It's about the size of a 1-liter water bottle. I was thinking about different bad scenarios. About bouncers kicking me out and people staring at me, pointing fingers and talking shit. I kept thinking about how to conceal the camera. I was running the backup story in my mind. All that didn't really help, I was even more nervous.

We get to the club and walk right in. No pat-downs, nothing. I just mumbled *"Gutten Abend,"* as a sort of greeting to the bouncer and just walk in.

Vini comes after me with a big grin.

"Good job, bro! That wasn't so bad, was it? Now you can breathe a little, haha."

We go to a corner that's not too busy. Dim lights, loud music, drunk people all around us. We're probably the only ones sober inside the club besides the staff. I see Max casually putting a microphone on under his shirt and taping it to his chest. It all seemed like I was playing some spying video game, and not like real life at all.

I take out the camera and lens and assemble it. I plug in the headphones in the camera with my shaky hands, turn on the receiver, and put it in my pocket. Then Vini shows me how to hold the camera in a very casual way, just next to my hip so the wires are mostly hidden, so long as I don't raise the camera too much.

"Ok, a few things you need to know. Firstly, RELAX. Nobody cares about you here, ok? You need to be as close to Max as possible, right next to him. In his face. Don't worry about his girl, or anybody else. Be like his shadow, always close, otherwise

you might miss the part where he opens the girl. Nobody will notice you. If they do, Max will handle it."

"Also, make sure you repeatedly check the exposure and focus levels manually, because the setting and the light changes even if you just take a few steps around the club. Always pay attention to what he's talking about, it will give you hints if he will move the girl etc. Lastly, if the sound cuts out it means you are not recording anymore, so fix that ASAP."

Max nods in agreement and then adds his own two cents:

"Look man, this is why I hired you. This is the most important part, this footage is very important. I'll use it in my upcoming product, and I'll show it to teach guys how to talk to girls. I'll use it to blow their misinformed reality away, so they can get on the road of self-improvement. This is why you are here, so don't fuck it up.

This is more important than me losing the set because of you, or you being caught. Make sure you do this right and you have all the attention on the camera at all times. No chatting with girls, no trolling, 100% focused. OK?"

"OK."

And so it starts. I feel super nervous, but I follow and film. I think everyone is watching me all the time. I sweat profusely and I'm a bundle of nerves, yet I film. I am like a shadow. Vini is with me all the time, which helps a lot. He tells me what angle to pick, he double-checks the manual settings I set and is there to chat with me while Max is in a set talking to some girl.

As time passes, I'm not nearly as nervous. In fact, I start to feel like a secret agent on a mission. It becomes fun and exciting rather quickly. Seeing Max in action and girls reacting to him. It's crazy, listening to his words and observing what happens. It's like watching an action film in the cinema, except I star in it too. I soon realize how nobody actually gives a fuck, even if I'm right next to them.

I think about how epic this is. I wanted to get better at game, and now I'm in a nightclub in Vienna, side by side with one of the world's best dating coaches. I listen to what he's saying, watch his actions. How he reacts to girls, how he looks at them. How the girls chase, and how blasé he is about all that.

It seems just like another day at the office for him. He's collecting phone numbers in most interactions, he kisses a girl or two just like that. Not all the girls like him and open up, but the difference between me and him was, well, he didn't care that much. He took the rejection with a smile on his face and continued on to the next girl. And it was funny, because some of those girls saw how chill he was after a rejection and started to chase him just because of that.

Anyway, I am close to all this action. I just pretend I'm on my phone or look away from them, and nobody even notices the big lens that is pointed in their direction all the time. My mind is absolutely blown, I'm unlocking a new level of understanding.

Then something funny happens, Max tells me to film Vini as he is in a set with this super hot blonde. I film it and get him kissing the girl on camera. It's crazy, she was super hot, and they couldn't have been talking for too long. I was filming with Vini at my side just a few minutes ago, and now the Brazilian is already making out with a hottie.

Wow, even Max's assistant had such a crazy level of game. That makes me think that I haven't seen much from Max yet. I am feeling more than ecstatic, only the first night filming and I'm getting crazy shots already. But that was nothing yet.

With Max at my side, we exit the club following Vini, who is clearly on a mission to pull the girl. We trail a few meters behind them. The girl is so engrossed with Vini she doesn't even notice us. I later learned that this is usually the case. People are so focused on themselves, or even better, on the interesting guy/girl they are talking to, that they don't notice the surroundings.

They enter a fast food place nearby. We stop, and then Max spots a window that looks towards where the two sit. He used to be an assistant and cameraman of another older RSD coach, so his camera skills are still very sharp.

We position the camera on the window, literally 30cm away from their faces and turn away, as if we're leaning on the wall and just chatting. In the meantime, the camera is getting everything. Except the sound, the mic was taped to Max. However, Vini had his own recording device under his shirt.

I was super nervous. It was one thing in the club, where everybody is drunk and dancing, and there are low lights and loud music. It was different here on the street. Again, I had the feeling that everyone was watching us. It was also cold, we had to follow the two without our jackets, in just our collared shirts, otherwise we would miss them.

Then Vini and the girl stood up; we wait till they pass us and then follow them. They are headed towards the cabs. I am super nervous, but it helps that Max is by my side, otherwise I would totally freak out. They get to the cabs and we stand a few meters away. With Max's help, I make sure the focus is good and zoom in a bit. I get excited for the magic moment.

However, for some reason, only the girl gets in the cab and drives off.

Vini joins us and explains that the girl had some job in the morning, or some bullshit story like that, and that's why he couldn't pull. Ah well, it happens to all of us. We go in and film for another half an hour before calling it a night at around 3am. I've been filming for about four hours now.

We take the night bus home, because we are only two stops away from the Airbnb. On the bus I notice I'm pretty tired, but I feel super excited as well. So many things happened, I literally can't believe my life at the moment. And then I spot a cute girl with pizza sitting close to us...

Chapter Eight
HANNAH PIZZA

Saturday, 3am, Night Bus

"That's pizza looks really, really fatty."

I add a big grin and look into her eyes.

"I like pizza, I don't mind."

I start to chat with her and she seems pretty cool. She's your typical cute girl. She's not super hot, but she's pretty. She has brown hair, nice oval-shaped face, full lips, bright eyes. I couldn't see her body much though because she was wearing a jacket. And another thing I could notice around her, was a sort of melancholic vibe. A vibe of a person who feels very deeply, almost too much, and I could relate to that.

Anyway, we joke around, from pizza to my German skills to Vienna's clubs. A few minutes pass, then she is starting to get off. I'm a bit sad she's leaving, but I smile and wave goodbye.

Then Max pokes me:

"What the fuck man, go after her. She clearly likes you, just go with her, be a gentleman, accompany her home. And then ask for the toilet or something, invite yourself in, you know how it goes."

Oh my god, that was totally out of my reality. Chat up a girl on the bus, then just follow her home after 3 minutes of talking to her? How creepy is that? However, Max was right. She really did seem into me, and I liked her too. And if I didn't do anything now, I might never see her again. To hell with it, let's see what will happen.

"Hey, wait up. I'll walk you home, you're pretty cool."

She turns, and has a slightly surprised look on her face:

"Don't expect anything tonight, I just want to go home and sleep."

"That's cool, I don't mind. I just wanna hang out a bit more."

"Okay!"

We start walking and pick up the chat from earlier. Within minutes, the connection is back. I guess that's what people call "chemistry" with someone. I tease her a bit, but we have some real conversation too. Time seems to fly as we're walking the streets of Vienna in the night.

To be honest, I don't remember the topics we talked through. I just remember how the energy was amazing, super light. I was absolutely free to be myself and I liked how she reacted to my flirting and advances. Sounds completely crazy, but we had an amazing connection in the

20 or 30 minutes that we walked.

We arrive to her flat. We stand in front of the door and continue chatting. Several times, I try to invite myself in.

"Can I have a glass of water? Can I use the toilet?"

She smiles, but refuses. None of us were in a rush to go separate ways though, so we continue chatting for about half an hour.

I don't know how, but at some point I started to touch her more. This time there was no game in my head, I just felt like doing it. I caressed her face with my palms. I could feel her trembling under my touch, we were speaking less and less and we were looking deep into each others eyes.

I kissed her neck. Something changed in her eyes. There was a deep look that I couldn't fully understand. The sexual tension was through the roof, there was electricity in the air. I had mixed feelings about this, but I couldn't say for sure what it meant.

I had a feeling that she needs this, that she's been without an intimate contact with a guy for some time. I could sense that because her feminine energy flourished, and I felt how she melted when I touched her. However, I also sensed that she was afraid. Afraid of the intimate contact, she's probably been hurt in the past.

A few amazing moments pass, mostly silence and looking into each other's eyes. Then she pulls out some lip balm and puts it on her lips. For some reason, I ask her to put it on my lips as well. It sounds super cheesy, but when she was putting lip balm on my lips, there was a 100% trust between us. That was fucking amazing. I was looking deep into her eyes as she was putting lip balm on my lips, super gentle, super caring. The time stopped.

And then I kissed her.

That was and remains one of the best kisses I ever had. Soft, gentle, and seeming to last forever.

We just stood there for some time. I tried to invite myself in again, but she again refused. She made no effort to leave or to go to bed, yet she still didn't want me to come in. It would be too much for her, I guess.

I liked her so much I just stood there too. As a man, you should always lead. If I decided that nothing more will happen that night, I should have kissed her goodbye and left. Instead, I just stood there and put the burden of decision-making on her. That was not right.

After some time, she finally says she really needs to go now, and she leaves. We kiss and hug goodbye, and I'm a bit sad to leave.

Sunday Evening

On Sunday evening, before we left Vienna, I met her again.

After 6pm we were finished with work for the day, and I asked Max if I could take the rest of the night off to meet that girl I really liked. He was cool with it, even better, he was happy about it.

I still remember the date, it was awesome. I met her at Vienna State Opera, and then we walked the streets of Vienna and just chatted. She even helped me film a video I was doing for my upcoming Youtube video channel called

BossLifeHacks. Then she showed me a nice coffee place for drinks later on, located on Vienna's main pedestrian street.

Amazing place, great energy and great connection, in the perfect atmosphere. Dim lights, lounge-type music, two glasses of alcohol, even though I don't usually drink.

However, throughout the date, I sensed she wasn't as open as when I first met her. I didn't understand. She wouldn't even want to hold my hand or kiss me, despite happily doing so the other night. No problem: I didn't get butt hurt, but just dismissed that as her being shy. However, inside I was burning with questions, why was this happening? We already kissed, so I didn't understand what the problem was now.

#**Butt Hurt**
A slang term for a guy who's acting like a little bitch. If a girl doesn't do as he likes, he starts making up drama and blaming her etc. Being butt hurt is never good, but happens to the best of us. Another word would be #**Needy**, as in "needing" the girl to do or not do something, and being emotionally dependent on that.

We actually talked about these topics as well. She told me how it's been months since she's been with a guy and that she's probably uncertain because she knows I will leave the next day. It made a lot of sense. She was very mature in that way.

"I think you are afraid, Hannah."

"I can see that, I can feel it. You enjoy spending time with me, as I do with you. And to me it seems like you crave the connection, the contact, intimacy. I felt really strong emotions when caressing your face the other night. More than strong, it was out

of this world.

Yet, I think you're closing yourself down, because you're afraid of being hurt again. I don't mean to sound like a dick, but I really believe that. I think vulnerability is key, and only by opening up to the pain, you can truly heal. And on top of that, if you close yourself to pain, you close yourself to happiness too, it's a double-edged sword."

"Plus, you look so fucking beautiful right now, sitting in front of me, with your big, sad eyes and your wavy brown hair, oh my god!"

Pretty deep shit, right?

But ah well, never try to convince a girl logically, it doesn't work like that. Never argue. Never explain too much. No matter how much your logical guy side wants to do it, it doesn't work like that, we're just different in energies. Hug her, tease her, playfully push her away, kiss her. But don't argue.

After the bar, I wanted to walk her home again. She would not let me. Probably because it took so long to say goodbye the last time. Not only because of the time, but because it was difficult.

And then, despite trying not to, I got butt hurt. She wanted to give me a hug and kiss goodbye and then leave by herself. I refused to give her the hug and kiss. She watched me in disbelief. She tried again and I refused again. I was doing what we call a takeaway.

#Takeaway
When a girl doesn't do what you want her to, you withdraw most of, or all of your attention. Complete

emotional withdrawal. That can sting way more than words. And that's why it works. It's highly manipulative, so special care needs to be taken when using this. Better yet, don't use it at all.

I could see tears in her eyes as she walked away. I was hurt too. A lot. And I felt really bad. I stood there for some time, trying to figure out if I did the right thing - trying to emotionally press her because I believed that by her opening up more, that could actually help heal her wounds.

And even though my hypothesis was probably true, it was still an incredibly dickish move. I ran after her.

"Hannah, wait up. Look, I'm sorry. I was being a dick, I'm really sorry."

I had tears in my eyes at this point.

I'm quite an emotional guy to be honest, but still. What a sight. Both of us crying there on a Sunday night, midnight, the middle of Vienna's busiest pedestrian street, which was completely empty at the time. You can imagine the intensity of the emotions.

"Why are you crying?" she asks, tears in her eyes.

"Because I really like you. And because I was being really mean to you. I'm sorry."

She sees I'm authentic, and she accepts the apology. With tears on our cheeks, we hug. I say that I hope I'll see her again sometime, and she wishes me a safe journey.

I watch her leave, and then leave myself.

I still continue to text occasionally with her for more than half a year. Haven't managed to meet up with her again, but I'm pretty certain I will one day.

Chapter Nine
COPENHAGEN,
BLONDES, AND
FAKE BUS TICKETS

Copenhagen, October 2015

Next day, we flew to Copenhagen.

Copenhagen is a very nice city to live in. People are... happy. At least from what I could see. There are no beggars on the streets, everything is more or less clean, everything works and days pass by quite calmly. There's even a weed-legal zone in the city (Christiania) where masked men sell you dope. And even that's calm. It might all be just a façade, but I liked it.

The next amazing thing were blondes everywhere. I don't know what nature did to women there, but they were simply beautiful. Probably only Swedish girls can match them. And they're pretty cool too. You see, when you have a hot girl in US or Germany, she might become a bit full of herself. Not every girl, mind you, but more than a few. And just because she's hot. In Copenhagen, every girl is hot, so there was no need to be special.

There were only two downsides. The weather, which was not even too bad for the time of the year, and the cost of living. See, at some point we had a chat with an African Uber driver, he had moved to Copenhagen a few years ago. You could see it on his face when he said winters are tough. Long months of frost and cold and not that much sun.

And the prices? I immediately noticed that Vini was an experienced traveller, and since none of us were getting paid yet, I quickly learned some effective ways of reducing my expenses. I started to eat beans. And a lot of pasta. Gotta love the pasta. And I started to use the "free" public transport.

See, in some cities, you can just use the metro (underground) without paying. The only trick is to keep calm. For example, Vienna and Berlin are my favorites, I (and most other people, even residents) never buy tickets there. But you can easily do same with Zurich's trams too. From back in the day I remember nobody paid in Belgrade either. The consequences are rare.

Copenhagen is a bit trickier. The metro can normally be used without a ticket, whereas buses (and we needed a bus from our place) are different. You either pay the driver, show him your actual ticket, or show him your mobile ticket (hint, hint).

So what did Vini and I do? We downloaded a sample ticket from the web and saved it in our gallery in the phone. Every time we entered the bus, we would just flash the phone at the driver (like all other people who probably had tickets) and he would just nod his head and let us in. The numbers (date and time) were really small and it looked like we had real tickets.

That was the first time I learned how far you can get by keeping it cool. And I don't mean any immoral, criminal stuff here. For example, you can get into an elite night club through firm eye contact and keeping it cool (you need to dress the part too). You can take an extra piece of hand luggage on the plane or go in last and then pick any free seat you want. Unless it's fully booked, nobody will check it.

Copenhagen, January 2016

When I visited Copenhagen half a year later, still on tour, just before going to the USA, I had an incident. It was about 4am, I am in the metro on my way home. As it happens, I'm chatting up a girl. We both had a mediocre night and were actually considering having a drink before we both went home. Well, I was considering that, but I had a feeling she wouldn't mind. However, one stop before ours, the ticket guys come.

Fuck.

"Sir, do you have a ticket?"

"Nope. "

"Miss, are you with him?"

"Nope."

Busted! So very quickly, I lost my girl and I was also

getting fined. Ah well, time to become a gangster, I guess.

"Sir, do you have any ID on you?"

"Nope."

"Could you check your pockets please?" (me obviously having a wallet in my pocket)

"I told you, I don't have my ID. I never take it out with me, I don't want to lose it."

"Sir, we'll need to call the police then."

"Okay, that's cool."

They accompany me out of the metro. It was 4.30 am and the guys were both clearly tired. I knew they were probably not going to call the police at 4.30 am because some random dude in a metro didn't have a ticket.

Then I give them my name - Peter Lewis, and then sign the paper they hand me. Almost signed as Bostjan, haha. They give me a ticket for $100 and ask me to go to the post office and pay it the next day.

We all knew that was not going to happen, but I still nodded my head.

So look, you can get away with a lot of things if you know how to handle it. I'm not saying you should always skip the line and never pay for your public ride tickets. I'm just saying that if you travel the world on a budget, there are ways to save money besides eating beans.

And then I went home. I walked to an extra metro stop

twenty minutes farther away, but with a little more "swagga" to my walk.

Chapter Ten
THE BOOTCAMP
BEGINS

Copenhagen, October 2015

The lights are flashing everywhere. Blue, green, white.
Pitch black. It's very loud. We're in what Max would later
on call the "second half of the night." You see people
dancing, drinking, making out. Everybody is drunk.
Except us, and maybe the staff.

I hold a $5,000 professional DSLR camera in my hand and
try to focus on Max while he's talking to a girl. I'm happy I
have in-ear headphones because they block out some of
the loud music. I can also hear what Max is saying.

One student is very close and is observing and listening.
The other two students are with Vini, who is explaining
something to them. We are in the middle of a program
called "The Bootcamp," which is an intensive, three-day
program where guys pay a lot of money to Max so he
teaches them how to meet attractive women.

I still couldn't believe where I was. I was in some posh club in Copenhagen with one of the best dating coaches in the world. It was beyond exciting. It was thrilling, it was gangster, it was like being in a movie. Or better yet, it's like being a NBA fan and then playing on Kobe's team. Like passing him the ball so he can dunk it and stuff.

Dude, it was seriously mind blowing.

I saw Max opening and flirting with these HOT girls that I would not have the balls to even talk to back then. Literally, a lot of the girls in Copenhagen, and well, most of the Northern Europe, were so hot, I would get nervous by just looking at them. I needed to spend a lot of time around Max to eventually being able to come up to them and not say something completely stupid or awkward.

After a while, Max signals to me and Vini, and we find all the students and regroup in the outside smoking area, where it's easier to talk.

"Jared, look, what the fuck have I been telling you all night? You need to be louder, man. There's a million things that can distract a girl in the night club, and if she can't hear you, you can be sure as hell she won't be coming home with you after the night ends. Look, I know you think you're yelling in your own head, but you're not. You need to be louder, OK?"

That's Max when he's frustrated at the Bootcamp. It only happens when the students repeatedly won't listen to what he says. Which is a shame. Because when I see students listening, they get results too. They get make outs, they pull. More importantly, they get the real-world experience of talking and interacting with girls. And sooner or later, they realize they don't suck as much as they thought they did.

"Alright guys, it's 2am, we'll do a bit of street game before I let you go for tonight. This is what we call the third half of the night. Yes, you heard me right. The third half of the night. This is where the energy is the highest. Imagine it like it's a mini New Year's Eve. There's magic in the night, and everybody likes an awesome movie ending, right?

Guys have been buying the girls drinks, the girls have been dancing, and enjoying themselves. The girl doesn't just want to go get food and go home, she wants to go home with a cool guy. However, no cool guy was brave enough to pull the trigger and lead her.

But be careful, because generally, only drunk people and beggars talk to girls on the street at this time of the night. So you need to show them you're not that. You need to show them you're normal. Just ask her how her night was, the line doesn't matter.

Don't try to stop her, just walk with her. Also, walk a little in front of her, not behind. If you walk behind her it's creepy and she will feel like you're stalking her. NEVER, EVER, touch or grab her when on the street. Be nice, smile, and be super casual.

Just be cool and talk to her. Tell her how your night was, which club you went to. Be a little funny, take your time. When you guys connect for a bit, offer her to walk her home, or to a cab, like a gentleman. And then improvise from then, go for the number, or suggest a quick drink or a snack, you never know."

I started to absorb that knowledge. Make no mistake, I had pretty decent game before that, but this was on another level. I quickly noticed that even though he was only 25 years old at the time, Max had a LOT of experience with women. On top of that, he was being completely genuine.

There were no scripted lines that he would teach the guys, he had what he called "Natural Game." It would all be very simple. Eye contact, loud voice. Talking without filters, listening to the girl, not just trying to bust out a few scripted lines. Making a move when the time is right, taking everything lightly and not being too outcome-dependent. We could all clearly see this behavior in his game too.

He seemed to always know what to do, what to say, where to move. He was paying attention to the environment, made sure the girl's friends were happy, knew exactly how and when to touch her to spice up the interaction. He knew how to withdraw his attention if she was a player herself, and how to make her laugh when things started to get boring. How to talk deeply and open up himself, so she would get in touch with his core.

In addition, maybe the most impressive thing I noticed was that when he talked to a girl, there was a sort of quiet intensity about him. I saw that on the first night we gamed together, and I saw it more and more. The intensity in the way he and the girl looked at each other. The eye contact that spoke without words, the communication beyond what words can say. Something I, for the most part, didn't have yet. I didn't know it then, but I got to know it later on. It was the silent life experience.

The experience of sleeping with hundreds of beautiful women. The experience of dealing with life when it gives you a lot of shit. The experience of dealing with unknown situations daily, the experience of getting hurt, and the experience of having hundreds applaud you.

And women, well, they have an amazing intuition. This is

the sort of experience that women will sense in a guy very quickly. They will notice this about you when you talk to them, they will read it from your eyes.

There is no way to fake it.

Chapter Eleven
PROJECT NIGHT, BATTLESTAR GALACTICA

The Flat of Max's Host, Copenhagen, October 2015

"Ladies and Gentlemen, Welcome to the Battlestar Galactica project night. Bring a lot of healthy snacks, coffee and/or green tea, your Macbook Pro, and some work you need to get done. Then plug yourself into the Matrix and grind hardcore for about 8 hours till 3 in the morning.

Oh, by the way, I got upgraded to a Macbook Pro. I tried to make the video editing software run on my old computer, but the laptop was just too slow. So the next day, back in Vienna, Max simply took me to the shop, cashed out 2500€, and bought me a MacBook Pro.

"Here, bro, you'll need this for the editing, and I'll need it for the next assistant at some point in the future anyway, so it's an investment. But you can keep it for now. Take good care of it."

That was so sick, oh my god. First of all, there was a big boss factor to that, he just walked into the store and spent 2.5k just like that. I wasn't living in a world where that was a reality yet. I'd research the shit out of that and spend months saving, and then buy it, but only if I was convinced it truly is the best value for money, etc.

He just walked into the store and bought the damn thing.

And to be honest, he was being really kind too. In the job description, it was mentioned I'd need a fast laptop. Well, I obviously didn't have one. He never said a word about that. He just bought the MacBook. I was incredibly grateful in that moment and my respect for him grew by a ton.

Anyway, back to the project night.

We would do a project night one-to-three nights a week. If you want to know what the usual day of an RSD coach or his assistants looks like, well, this is a big part of it. Project night is just a fancy name for hardcore work, mostly video editing. Max would edit his content videos, Vini would help him with that or even fix his color correction. My task was to first learn, and then do the censoring for Max's in-field videos.

You know when you see a blurred face in a video? Well, that's me. And guess what, it takes a lot of time. For example, there are typically 24 frames per second in your average video, and you need to reposition the censor bar or circle for every frame when the person moves their head.

Which means 24 click and drags for each second of the video. Which means about two-to-four hours for every one minute of censoring, depending on the difficulty. Later on I could do it even faster, but it still took a lot of time.

See, the good thing about monotonous work such as censoring is that you can multitask. As advised by Max, I would normally listen to a good audiobook or a Youtube speech while censoring. After a few hours when I got really tired I would just blast deep vocal House music to get a little more energy and continue to bust censoring out.

And a strange thing happens when you work this focused and this hard. You actually get high off of work. A few hours in, we would start to laugh like retards for no reason. Or we would start sending funny .gifs (little moving pictures) to the other two guys. Or post a really funny Facebook status. Or some other random funny shit.

But the thing is, you are so focused for so long that your brain cannot really cope with it, so you experience something similar to a high. Natural and healthy. Not to mention SUPER productive. Pretty cool, I never experienced that before, I used to hate work of this nature and couldn't really focus for more than 30min at a time. This helped.

And I started to love project nights.

Did I have the best work ever with the censoring? Hardly. However, I accepted it, it's a part of what I do and I have to get this done before more fun stuff happens. Plus, I can add some extra value with audio books. After accepting that, a strange thing happened.

I entered a mindset called "flow state." It's a phenomenon that you probably know too. It's when you are super focused and so emerged in an activity that time just flies by. Its's almost a meditative experience. You don't think about tomorrow or yesterday, or about that girl, or even about how hungry you are. You are just immersed in the moment and one with the activity... or well, with the censoring in my case, haha. And the best thing about it? You produce a lot of value too.

And then when your buddies have your back and do the same, it's just awesome; mutual motivation on steroids. When one person would get tired, he'd get motivated by the others and vice versa.

And I can hear the critics already, *"But Bostjan, you did all of this for free, you even spent your own money."*

Yes, that's true.

However, I also got the habit down now. I am now able to launch a project night on my own, or even better, with some friends. And to have the skill set that allows you to put in full nights of work after your regular day is over, that is worth way more than any amount of money.

After each editing session, and even after every night of filming, Max would do something simple, yet really cool.

"Thanks for today, bro, I appreciate it."

Following was a fist bump, to both me and Vini.

Now, he didn't need to do that, I'd still do all the work. But he chose to do that. And it made me feel special. It made all the hard work easier, and it made me feel appreciated. Which is one of the things that a lot of employers miss. They don't make you feel important and needed, which is worth far more than money. And I learned that too.

Anyway, project Battlestar Galactica is DONE.

P.S

"DONE" in caps has a sort of sentimental value. It's the codename of a finished project, be it video, the whole night, or whatever, so there's a sigh of relief coming out every time I write it.

Chapter Twelve
STRAIGHT OUT OF OSLO FREE TOUR

Oslo, October 2015

Oslo was the first time I got sick. It didn't take me too long, I hadn't even been on tour three weeks yet. However, I am not surprised. We lived a hardcore lifestyle, up until 4am or 5am every day, sleep until about 12pm. Work more or less all day, every day, fly to a new country every week.

We'd hit the gym regularly too. One of the first tasks in a new country, either Monday night after flight or Tuesday morning, would be searching up the local gyms and checking out their layout and application process.

Most of the time we could actually get free one week trial sessions, I just had to search for it. When we couldn't find any free sessions, Max would usually pay the fee for Vini and I. You can imagine we were grateful, because I doubt we'd buy them ourselves.

Anyway, it's really easy to lose balance on tour. A day of junk food, missed exercise, or ploughing through with not enough sleep can throw you out of sync, and health. So it happened to me quite early. I got sick. And it fucking sucked.

At first I started to be angry with myself. I couldn't work. I know Max and Vini already had respect for me, but I still really wanted to prove myself. Another thing is, a really good Slovenian friend of mine visited from another Norwegian city where she lived. And I couldn't even meet her because I felt like shit.

Damn.

But then I remembered the Buddhist philosophy of accepting things as they are. I'm sick, fuck it. What can I do with it? I took two painkillers, ate some fruit, and checked if I had some movies on my computer. I found a pirated copy of *"Straight out of Compton."* So I watched the sick movie and felt like a gangster for a few hours.

Then I just did the regular thing when you are sick. A lot of sleep, fluids and feeling like shit. And mega doses of vitamins and other supplements – N-Acetyl-Cysteine (NAC) is really good for your immune system, check it out. My host was super cool too, he gave me a lot of space and was mostly out of the flat, which I really appreciated. And then luckily, after two days I was somewhat cool again.

I even got to meet my friend and chill for a whole afternoon with her. It's funny, because she is one of my few female friends that I don't want to bang. I really appreciate her friendship and am super grateful to have her by my side. I remember I Skyped with her a few times when I was feeling really low and she always helped me out – it's awesome to have cool female friends as a guy.

I got well just in time, because we ran our first Free Tour on Thursday. It would always be a Thursday.

Me and Vini arrived two hours before the scheduled time of the speech. We checked in at the hotel desk and were shown to the big seminar room. In the next two hours, we prepared everything.

We met the volunteers and I listened and learned how Vini explained their roles to them. They would help us meet and greet the visitors, prepare the hall, and sell Max's paid premium program later on.

Then we rearranged the chairs so they matched the projected number of visitors, made sure that the sound system was working as it should, and balanced the projector so it worked perfectly. We made sure the AC was working properly, since it could get really hot in a room packed with people. Lastly, we'd shoot a picture of the place setup to Max, who would confirm that everything looks good.

Since we still had some time and everything was set up and ready, we relaxed a bit. We blasted some of our favorite songs on Youtube and played funny videos on the projector.

I would always chat with some volunteers too, they are always super cool guys. I mean, obviously, if you volunteer to help out with something just because you think that's a nice thing to do, you're already cool by definition. It's an admirable personal trait, wanting to help someone without wanting anything in return.

Anyway, Max enters about 30min before the speech, double-checks if everything is good. Vini does the test run with the main camera. He will be operating the main shot from the middle of the audience, My job is to regularly check the back shot and organize the volunteers towards the end of the program. Having two shots of the same speech would allow us to create a double-angled video after. This was some professional videography, not some rookie BS.

While the seminar room fills, we shoot the shit with Max. He just jokes around, imitates Borat Sagdiyev, and tells me and Vini about his favorite metal song he just heard. It's all kind of random, but I fall in quickly, we all bust out some jokes and just hang out in the back as the seminar room starts filling.

I later on learned that this process helps Max to get ready for the speech. It's an activity that helps you put your mind at ease, to become less stifled and to activate your speech organs. Puts you in a more social mode.

Then Max goes farther to the back, so he's out of sight, and Vini moves to the front. I dim the lights and Vini plays the intro, basically a short and cool video of Max. After the video plays out, Vini returns to the middle, I turn on the lights and Max comes on stage. People start clapping and cheering like crazy, he looks like a rock star at the moment.

Once the cheering calms down, Max starts to speak. First, he gets a feel of the audience, where they are all from, how many of them have been to other RSD events before and so on. Then he gives them the *"How I Discovered Game"* story.

It's a good story, very personal and straight forward. It's

basically a tale of a shy nerdy Austrian guy from a little cow-town, who discovers the hidden world of the game, and starts to get better with women, all up until he achieves the RSD Executive Coach position, flying all around the world helping guys get more confident around women.

I laugh at some points and it resonates with me a lot. I guess all guys into game have similar journeys. Most of us start of as a dude who sucks with girls and just wants a nice girl around him, and then a whole world of adventure opens.

After that he starts the question and answer session, and then just goes on a rant when he gets a good question that resonates. He addresses all sorts of worries, from how to get fit, to what to text her, to what sort of books he reads. Questions regarding lifestyle, game theory, the way women think. Even some random questions about fantasy games and movies, everything goes.

The guys there really receive a lot of value. Basically it's a free speech that is tailored to their wants and needs. In addition, it's an awesome place for networking and making new friends, business partners, wings. You see, at these events you'd meet people who are actively trying to improve themselves and their lives. And that's rare.

I notice he more or less freestyles the whole thing, which tells me he's done it before. He's very experienced in public speaking. There's no way you can just pull a three-hour speech out of your head in front of a large audience without prior practice. I learned a lot from all those free tours.

In the end he sells in a very smart way.

After the rant, he talks about his paid, premium program, the Hot Seat. A 10-hour long game theory analysis. He depicts how he literally takes guys by the hand, and shows them every point in the interaction, from meeting to dating, to sex and relationships.

All questions are answered and all theory is explained. It costs a few hundred dollars. The bits of video material he shows are really good. Street kiss of a super hot girl in two minutes. Pulling a girl from the club to cab and later on hotel without saying a word. A girl grabbing his dick in a club and then following him to the toilet. Guys are blown away.

Then he presses upon audience pain points:

"Do you not have the results with women that you want to have? Are you still unsure of what to say, what to do? Have you had enough of just watching videos of other people? Do you want to have pretty girls around in your life?"

Next off, he creates a beautiful image.

"The life I want to have is great. I want to wake up next to a beautiful girl. Super skinny, long blonde hair, tight petite ass. She smells of strawberries. She rubs herself again my dick and says: "One more time baby, please." I answer: "Oh, I'm sorry baby, I think 5 times was enough..."

Then he uses this leverage to inspire action:

"Are you an action taker? Do you want to take your game to a new level? Do you want to get that perfect 10 that you always wanted to? Stand up! STAND UP!"

I see a couple of guys standing up. And some more follow.

"Stand up, and go see our team in the back. The Hot Seat will bring you all the theory you ever need, then you just need to take action. Stand up now, and go see our team in the back and they'll help you sign up."

"I'll be in the back, available to answer all your questions and to take pictures. Everybody, thanks for coming and may the force be with you!"

About 15 guys come to the sales table, more follow. Max is answering questions and taking pictures. The volunteers, Vini, and I are signing the guys up for the Hot Seat. It's quite manic at points, making sure everybody is catered to, sign up forms flying in the air, flashes in the back from the picture taking, people chatting, smiling, there's a buzzing energy in the air.

I'm taking mental notes all the time, this excites me. The selling, providing value, personal growth, business, the good life. The smiles of people, the buzzing energy, the rockstar status. The networking and group dynamics, the sharing of one's story and how motivating it can be to the others.

It's so awesome, because I know the guys got inspired. Hell, I got inspired every time, and I'd heard that speech dozens of times, and it still got to me. It motivated you. I was certain that most of those guys will go out that night and try their best to meet the girls they like. I was certain they will reflect about their life and the stage they are at. I was certain, that from now on, they will put a little more effort in becoming a better person.

After we finish up, Max goes to the toilet, changes into nice club clothes, eats a protein snack, finds and takes the three of his students, and heads straight to the Bootcamp venue. Sometimes I wondered how he did all of that. First a 4-hour speech, then straight into the intensive 5-hour private infield coaching. Vini and I take some time to clean up, pack the gear, thank the volunteers, and take a cab back to our place.

We got to the Free Tour hotel around 4 pm. It's about 11 pm when we come home. We quickly grab a bite, I take the camera gear, and we Uber it back to the Bootcamp location. We're in the club before midnight and the filming begins.

I get the feeling that it's gonna be a long night.

Chapter Thirteen
I'M IN HIS CASA

Lay Report, October 2015

Inner Circle Oslo Facebook Group

Saturday Evening. Heading out with the crew and a student to one of Oslo's poshest night clubs. I got kicked out (very politely though) the night before, so we decide we won't do any filming that night.

Sweet, it means I can actually game once for a change. We chill for a bit as the student is being instructed. Then all of us pop into sets left and right, I bring a few girls to the guys and vice versa.

Basically, most of the Nordic guys are super chody (meaning they are bad with girls), so all the girls open really well.

#Chode
Is a guy who is afraid of being a guy. He's afraid to show that he likes a girl, he thinks liking sex is bad, he feels bad about expressing what he really feels and wants. A lot of this is to blame on the whole society's instruction of what a cool guy

should be, but not all of it. We also call chode pretty much any guy who does not know about the game or lacks game.

Anyway, the pimping continues. If the girls start to lose interest, or have friends that need attention, I toss them to Max, Vini, or the student. Or if I know Max or Vini really like a certain type of girl I introduce her to them right off the bat. Nothing special, a regular night out, except I still can't believe the general hotness of girls here.

Some hot Turkish girl hooks really well. She gives me plenty of shit:

"Do you say this to every girl?" "You're a little short for me, huh?"

However, I don't give in, and appear unaffected, like a boss (she's taller by 15cm too, haha). She's about to leave so I number-close and let her go.

#Close
Close is an end-point stage in interaction between a guy and a girl. There's different closes, for example the number-close, or #close, kiss-close. There's the old school slang term f-close, which means a fuck-close. You also have a Facebook-close or basically any other close you can think of.

Everyone is in sets now. I see the student hooking some chick well, but she has a friend. So I go wing him on the dance floor. It's super fun actually. The other girl doesn't really find me attractive (thought she might like a younger stud) but I still keep her happy. A few well-timed jokes, a compliment or two, and just being crazy and fun.

I do that for about 30min and then ask Vini if he could take over so I can game for a bit myself. He doesn't mind... so I go crazy!

Keep in mind, that was the first night in about 3 weeks I could actually let go, not needing to think about filming and actually game a bit for myself in the prime time. Otherwise I'd only get to game after 3am, when Max either pulled or went home and the filming stopped.

This was an epic night. Max bought Vini and I a beer each.

"It's Frank's birthday today."

Frank was Max's previous assistant. I thought that was super cool too, they were still in touch. Frank wasn't just some sort of cheap unpaid labor for Max, as some people try to depict us assistants. So we have a beer (Max doesn't, since he's still running the Bootcamp) and we have some fun.

I have a really good picture of the three of us from that night. Max has some sort of fluorescent necklace he got from some girl, Vini is wearing his black shades in the club like a total gangster, and I rock my beer, quite casually. Everyone's looking slick in button-up shirts.

Truly a dream team.

I'm super in state and make some flirty eye contact with chicks dancing around me then I open a two-set with some random shit. No wait, actually it was:

"Are you from Norway?"

Again they hook super effortlessly. It's so easy here, thank you chodes, haha.

#In/Out Of State
When you're in state, you feel amazing. You felt it before in your life before too. Maybe during sports, your job, at a game. It's

when everything seems to click. It's when you open girls and they all hook. It's when you get make outs just like that. It's when you have zero fear and feel invincible. How do you reach that? Usually it's a process of talking to so many girls that you don't care anymore. You let go of your fears and restrictions and just become truly genuine and in the moment. But there's random factors too. It's quite hard to explain.

"No, I'm Spanish."

I high-five her and then bust out my Spanish language knowledge to her:

"Como fue con la chica que te follaste anoche?"

Not sure if this is the correct way of writing it, but it should be slang for "How was the girl you fucked yesterday?"

It's very ballsy, but she can see it in my eyes and in my smile that I'm not being a dick, I'm just having some fun and trolling around.

She laughs her ass off, and we exchange a few more sentences and then dance. I introduce myself to her friend shortly and continue dancing - no fancy moves, just two-stepping. See, I'm a breakdancer. I know how to dance pretty well, but that rarely got me laid. So I just prefer to focus on the girl and our interaction, rather than trying to impress her with my dancing.

The brunette Spanish girl is nice. She is shorter than myself, with a very tight body, great ass, small breasts, curly brown hair, and big brown eyes. Everyone who knows me knows that I have a thing for curly hair.

It's just irresistibly sexy to me. Straight hair is cool, but not nearly as erotic as curls for me. I like her outwards energy too, she's quick to laugh, quick to show whether she likes you or not, very genuine. I like that.

Then her friend goes to get a drink, a good sign that she's not afraid to leave my girl alone with me. Plus, I started to get the idea that these two were on a cock mission tonight. Then I pull my girl in to dance closer with me, she likes it.

She grinds her tight little ass on my pelvis hardcore and it gets pretty hot. I actually move away a bit to increase the tension and she willingly comes back for more. I start feeling a boner inside of my pants.

We dance for about five more minutes. I can see her staring lustily in my eyes. I knew I could and probably should wait a bit more, but she has an amazingly sexy vibe about her.

I kiss her neck and then her lips, but not for too long, I leave her wanting more...While dancing I firmly touch her shoulders and sides of body. Girls love it when you firmly squeeze their shoulders and the sides of body.

You can do the same with arms, legs, and after all that is checked, then you go for boobs and ass. Most guys just drunkenly go for boobs & ass first. Fuck that. Take time with it, discover what she likes. The foreplay starts the moment you see her.

And while I do that, I pay attention to her reactions. If at any point she'd show even a sliver of discomfort, I'd stop. However, I could feel her breathing quicken, I could see her looking deep into my eyes, I could feel her grasping my hands stronger, and digging her fingernails in my arms. She grinds on my pelvis with more force.

Her friend comes back and smiles. She approves, another great sign! All this was maybe 30 minutes into the interaction; it's not always this fast, but it happens sometimes. I remember that my wings might need me at some point so I tell the 2 girls:

"Come meet my friends," and lead the two girls to our group, which now consists of Max, Vini, the student, and his two girls.

So I dance with my girl a bit more, Max jumps on her blonde friend and then quickly isolates her (well done, Max). Vini is around too, to keep the friend of the student's girl busy, so everyone is happy. We dance and have some fun, I can't help but laugh noticing Vini still keeping his black shades on.

#Isolate
When you move a girl to the bar or some other area of the club where you two can have a conversation. For example, if she's around her friends, it's a lot less likely she'll be okay with you two kissing, because all the friends might judge her. If you guys are alone, that's not an issue.

I start to seed the pull.

#Seed the Pull
When you start making future plans for the night with the girl. Either mentioning the two of you might get some food later on, or check out a movie, or get a drink, or have a walk. Basically, anything that signals you want to spend more time with her. So when the clubs closes, or when you make a move, she kinda knows and she's not surprised.

"We'll have some tea later, I have super amazing Rooibos tea at home."

"Cool, I like tea."

Nice! This girl loved me and was down to have some sexy-time tonight. All I had to do is relax and not fuck anything up.

Then after about 10 more minutes, when I suggest leaving, she's unsure:

"But my friend..."

I tell her that it's cool and she has her number anyway. But she insists. Okay, no problem. We go to find her friend, who is not with Max anymore (he later tells me he ditched her because she was being too difficult, can't blame him).

Then my girl wants to dance some more. Well, OK, no rush. Let's dance more. Soon her friend jumps on some other dude and my girl wants to "save her," meaning pulling her away from the guy. I stop her and tell her:

"What the fuck, let her have some fun, girl, she allowed you the same, so be cool! She clearly likes the guy, and the guy likes her too, there's nothing wrong with that."

She agrees and just dances and kisses me more.

I WhatsApp Max and Vini to ask if it's cool if I go for the pull and they say go for it. Sweet! Then I know it's pull-the-trigger time.

"Let's go."

"I wanna dance."

In my mind I'm like: "Here we go, the shit starts..."

"Food. Come, we'll be back soon. I'm really hungry."

She gives in to my certainty and comes with, and waits in the coat line while I take a piss. We grab our coats, and then we get out, hand in hand.

I lead hard: "This way!" and walk with her towards where I think it's the right way. Now the trick is that it's 2am, my host has the flat keys and he works till 4am in some bar. The flat is a 15 minute walk away from where me and the girl are, and my host's bar is even further.

No way I can do this much walking with her. Her mood will drop and once we get back to the flat she will either be sleepy, hungry, or having second thoughts about the whole thing: the social conditioning will kick in.

Meaning she will start to wonder if she's doing the right thing, thinking about if her friends will judge her, if sleeping with a guy she likes but hasn't known for too long makes her a slut. All these difficult questions that women need to face.

It's so unfair. If a guy is with a lot of girls, it's good, he's considered a player. If a girl is with a lot of guys, she's a slut. I hate this, but sadly, most people still think like that.

We start walking and then I'm like, "Actually, let's take a taxi." I stop one right there and get in without looking back. She's a bit confused, but comes in. All throughout I bust jokes and talk a lot, to make sure she's comfortable. She relaxes a bit and joins in the banter, so all good, we have our own little party bubble again. We laugh, talk and giggle.

We stalk some people on Facebook while driving, we listen to some music, there's an awesome vibe. One little part of me deep inside still can't believe what's happening and is screaming on the inside, "Ohhhh myyyy gooooood...."

We get to the bar, I tell her to wait in the cab and leave my phone with her to stalk more people on Facebook. That also makes her more comfortable, if I trust her with my phone, I've gotta be cool, right?

The taxi driver is a moron and stops too far away, so I run to the bar, get keys, high-five my host, and run back. Fuck, where is the cab? Turns out that the driver parked in an alley close by. I run around a bit, finally find them, and then give him the flat address.

Finally, we get to the flat. I pay the driver. Damn, it was expensive and I was already over my weekly budget. But what the hell, haha. I bring her up. Again, I talk throughout to avoid the silent awkwardness. We come into the flat, I tell her to put on the lights while I go to get some water from the kitchen.

Then we chill on the sofa and watch some clips on Youtube. I try to kiss her, but she doesn't want to. Cool, I don't push it, we watch more Youtube. I show her my breakdancing video, we talk more, she's becoming more comfortable again. We kiss. She pulls back quickly, she's still not fully comfortable. I tell her:

"Look, I know this is kinda fast, but don't worry, no pressure, ok? We don't have to do anything you're not comfortable with. It's just that I like you. I like kissing you, I find you really sexy. I want to touch you more, I want to hear you breathe heavy, I want to look deep into your eyes and hold you tight. But if I ever cross the line, just tell me, and I'll stop. Cool?"

She agrees and looks a bit more relaxed now. Then I remember it was cool dancing with her, and we both liked that. So I play some slow music and ask her to stand up. I play some dance music and we start to dance.

The dancing is really good. We dance slow and passionate, close to one another, so we can feel each other's body. I gently touch her face and cheeks, hair. I ask her if she's enjoying her time with me, she says yes. She starts to get more and more comfortable.

I remove her jacket and we continue dancing. It's starting to get hot. After some time I remove my shirt and continue dancing. Then I say "Let's lie down for a bit." We do that and then I start to rub her pussy, followed by some gentle and passionate kissing. She's cool with that and starts to moan.

Just when I think everything is smooth, and that I've plowed through all the shit and can finally relax a bit, her friend calls. Dammit. They speak in Spanish. I don't get it. But I understood she was asked where she was and she said something along the lines of "in his casa" I begin to think that I might end up with blue balls.

But after a 3 minute conversation she's like "Ok, my friend is good."

She fully relaxes.

I proceed to kiss her passionately, our clothes start to fly off. Oh my god, her fit ass feels so fantastic, and it makes me really horny. And hearing her moan while I finger her, that is really arousing to me. Her body is flexing under my hands and I feel her petite and warm body in my hands.

Then I open a condom, and it happens again. My old friend, the limp dick.

FUCK! You again, really!?

After 2 weeks I finally get to have some sexy time again, and my dick is fucking with me again, fuck my life. Oh well, after the initial frustration I relax a little, start breathing, and just focus on the girl. How cool it is kissing her, how she feels under my arms, how she moans when I finger her, how she bites my neck.

Her big round brown eyes.

I think her ass did it for me this time. Just tightly gripping that petite ass steadily got me hard again. I put on a condom, and slowly enter her. She's really tight, so I go slow. She breaths heavy and lets out a few gasps as I penetrate her fully. Then we just continue to have amazing sex. This one was more gentle and passionate, I could not classify it as hardcore fucking.

After sex we cuddle and kiss more, I start to like this girl. After a while, we get dressed, it's getting late, or well, early, and my host will be coming home soon. I was crashing on a couch in his room, so I didn't want to have the girl there because it was trouble enough having a dude sleep next to you for a week.

I walked her home, fortunately she lived quite close. We chatted, cracked some more jokes, and had a really long and passionate kiss goodbye.

I return home and sleep like a baby.

Chapter Fourteen
THE HOT SEAT

Berlin, October 2015

We had our first Hot Seat in Berlin. The Hot Seat is a premium RSD product, it costs a few hundred dollars and it provides value that can't really be measured by money.

Vini and I prepared everything. There is a projector screen, sending blue light onto the canvas. You can hear dim metal music in the background. The room is full of guys, they've all found a seat. Everybody has their water, pens, and notepads ready.

Vini goes to the stage and plays the intro, I turn off the lights, and Max enters the room silently. People don't go as crazy here as they do during the Free Tour. The air is full of expectancy. Max sits down and plays the first clip. It's him opening some very hot girl in the middle of the street. And after three minutes, they are kissing. Now the guys go crazy and start clapping.

Welcome to the Hot Seat.

What to say. How to deal with your fears, how and when to touch her. What to do with guys in a set, how to pull to your place, how to pull to hers. What to do if she's not listening to you, how to pass her shit tests... And it went on, and on, and on. For 10 hours. With no breaks.

In those 10 hours, the guys there saw some spectacular sights. They saw Max pull a girl from the club to the cab using absolutely no words. They saw him kiss uncountable girls, and pull girls from the most difficult situations. They saw him kiss girls he had met on the street, during the daytime, only a few minutes before. They saw him talk continuously at a girl for more than five minutes, without her saying anything back, before she finally opened up.

It was a lot of work for Vini and I too, especially the preparation. We had to get up at 9am, and that's the morning after the Bootcamp that ran until 4am or 5am. Zombie mode, coffee required. Those mornings were really busy. However, once we had the seminar room set up with all the projectors, sound system, tables, and chairs, and had liaised with hotel staff and other little things, we could rest a bit.

I got very good at sleeping in unusual places. See, while Max was on his 10-hour rant, as long as either Vini or I were in the seminar room (in case Max needed anything), the other was able to chill. It was a regular sight to see me sleeping on some hotel lobby couch, or even on the floor if there was a nice floor mat. I got very good at sniffing out cozy, quiet places in hotels.

A hint here: go to a floor that is not busy, or even better, try to find an open room where nothing is happening. Along with unconventional spaces to sleep, you can find all kinds of other cool things in hotels. I found everything from free supplies of various teas to cakes, coffee and cool chocolate bars.

The last clip of the Hot Seat was my favorite, and most of the guys said the same. It was Max chatting up some tattooed girl. She was being a real bitch to him, but he was being super nice and persistent. And then you could see her shedding away the top layers of her protections and gradually opening up to him.

The footage stops and then Max goes on a rant about the interaction. We follow him overcoming a lot of obstacles and performing almost heroic deeds to finally end up alone with her in her room. However, the story ends with both of them completely opening up, crying, and, surprisingly, not having sex.

It was an intense, emotional speech. It was hard for me to hold back my tears the first couple of times I heard that. It was because I could relate. And I saw similar expressions on faces around me. Because the truth is, as Max would say in the speech,

"In the end, we are all just little boys who want to be loved."

That's why we all crave these adventures. That's why we seek the feminine, why we strive to become master seducers, why we want to have countless girls. Because somewhere deep down we were hurt. And all we want is for someone to love us.

Chapter Fifteen
ALEX AND SKYPE SEX

Berlin, October 2015

For this story, we need a bit of backstory.

Rewind to two months earlier. Back in London, just before I embarked on this crazy World Tour.

London, August 2015

At that time I was unemployed. I had just recently quit my job as a Problematic Youth Worker, because my boss was a moron. So I lived on savings, and tried out a lot of different things to make money. I felt a bit unsure and increasingly pressured, but also very free. A somewhat successful way to make some money was to be a street performer, using my breakdance and public speaking skills in Trafalgar Square. I also jumped onto every other opportunity I got.

So one time my friend Theodore offered me £100 for a day

of painting and, obviously, I was down. After we had finished, we headed towards the train station. I was supposed to be going on a date with a Polish girl I had met a week or so ago. She was hot, but living far away, and our initial interaction wasn't super amazing, so I wasn't sure if she saw me as friend or as a potential lover.

In the park not far from his house, two hot girls were walking towards us. I was feeling super happy and goofy because of the painting, and although I was running late for the train, I had to talk to them. I had no idea of how to open them. I just said the first thing that popped into my mind, unfiltered.

Besides, Eye contact and a good smile matter far more than the exact words.

"Hey!"

"Do you girls know how to play football?"

They laughed, gave me the Bambi eyes and stopped to chat with us. Obviously they didn't care much about football. Women have amazing natural social intuition, something that we guys need to work hard on to learn. So obviously, they knew we were hitting on them. Let the game begin!

They were both pretty, and as we later learned, from the Czech Republic. Interesting, most of the pretty girls I met in London were not actually British. It was a slow sunny Sunday, and the girls didn't seem to be in a rush. I figured they had time on their hands, so I told them that me and my buddy Theodore were on our way to the shop to get crisps and beers so we could sit in the park and celebrate a successful painting session. I told them they should totally joins us.

Soon afterwards we were all sitting in the park, listening to music, eating crisps, and drinking beer. First I decided on the blonde, because her English was better. I like it when girls understand and laugh at my stupid jokes. but after a while I switched to the brunette because I wanted to thank Theodore for hooking me up with the job. I also thought it would be funny to game a girl who spoke almost zero English.

I started to like this brunette girl named Alex though; she was kind of goofy. And then I learned she liked to dance as well. I was hooked, I love a girl who can dance.

I started to teach her basic breakdance moves and she was loving it. She was super good too, I was surprised. Then we made up a routine together (no, she's not the only girl I taught that routine to) and showed it to the other two. We got a round of applause and we all laughed and continues to chill together.

At some point I took my girl and walked off with her, telling the group we would back in five minutes because I needed to show her something.

I brought her to a cool stone bench in the park, sat behind her, and started to massage her. She told me that she was 19 and I noticed that she had a super hot, tight body. Frankly, she turned me on like crazy. I start to kiss her neck and can feel she is melting and getting turned on too. I try to kiss her but she gracefully turns her head and says *"Next time."* Damn, sometimes I feel like she gamed me.

Next time I met Alex we had a super romantic date in London. It was a few days before my flight to Vienna. It was awesome. I showed her my favorite casino and then we got some beer and chilled at the statue in front of Buckingham Palace. We listened to Youtube music videos, talked, hugged, and even took some pictures with some underage kids who were smoking cigarettes near to us.

Next I took her to the tube station. I told her that I wanted to take her home with me and cook her dinner. I could feel that she really wanted to come, but she explained that she needed to be home before midnight, which was in 20 minutes from then. She was an *au pair* (a nanny) and she had a deal with the family she worked for to be home before 12. Damn! We had a super long, passionate kiss goodbye. A few days later, I left London and went on the tour.

I kept in regular contact with this girl, even on tour. Every few days we would shoot each other some messages, a picture or two. Regardless of me hardcore-chasing new girls, I really appreciated something more constant: an ongoing connection with a super cool girl.

At some point when I was in Berlin, something really cool happened. I don't know exactly how it started, but we were chatting, you know, just texting back and forth. And somehow, our conversation would steer towards sexuality. I made some remarks about jerking off, and she teased me about it.

And then, I don't know how it actually happened, but I remember she sent me a hot picture of herself. She was wearing only underwear in a super sexy pose, standing with an arched back, her boobs showing in the perfect position.

I got SUPER horny. Like, you should see that picture.

Imagine a hot 19-year old girl with a super tight body, long, curly brown hair (remember, curls are my weakness), and an arched back so her perfect ass sticks out. On top of that, she was wearing some super sexy and very revealing underwear. Oh my god, I could feel my dick getting hard.

And to be honest, I was not used to getting pictures like that from girls. I knew girls sent pictures like that to guys, I saw it on my friends' phones. But I never got pictures like that. So this was really exciting, a hot girl is sending me sexy pictures of herself, shit, that's when you know life is becoming really good.

Max and Vini were editing next to me. We were in Max's Airbnb. But my mind was off work, I couldn't focus anymore. I sent her a message:

"Skype?"

She replied with her username.

I told the guys I'm gonna take a quick shower, took my laptop, and locked myself in the bathroom.

At first I felt kind of awkward; it would be the first time I had ever attempted the infamous "Skype sex." Even more awkward was the fact that we hadn't even had sex in real-life beforehand. Anyway, I put some music on, so the guys would not hear anything. Also, luckily, the bathroom was separated by 2 doors. Then I sit on the bath tub, put the laptop on the washing machine, and press "video call."

She answers, and she looks beautiful. Casually half-sitting, half-lying in the bed, in her pajamas, which is panties and a baggy T-shirt for most girls. I can clearly see the shape of her awesome tits through the shirt. I can see the passion in her eyes, despite the shitty image quality of Skype.

She can't speak, because her host parents are in the next room, but I can. I first awkwardly ask her how she is, and start it off as a chat. She texts back that she's well, but a bit bored, etc. After a minute, I start kicking myself internally.

"What the fuck bro, you Skyped her so you can ask her how she is? Really, dude? "

I get my shit together, and tell her how hot I think the picture she sent me was. I tell her it made me feel really horny, and that I have a boner. And the boner always helps, it makes the fear go away, it puts you in the moment.

"Baby, I want you to know how horny I am right now. If I was there, I would sit behind you, slowly brush your hair back, and then gently breathe onto your neck. You'd feel how hot my breath is, and it would arouse you. You'd feel the heat of my body behind you. Then I'd start to firmly grasp your shoulders, just like I did that time in the park.

I wouldn't stop there. I'd start kissing your neck, and then pulling your hair, gently, yet still strong enough that it would be super sexy and pleasurable. I'd touch the sides of your body, and I'd touch your ass. I'd feel you trembling under my hands."

I could see she was completely turned on. She was eating up every word I said, looking directly into me, and I could see her hands clasping the parts of her body. They run up and down her thighs, stomach, and breasts. I'm not sure if she did it on her own, or was just so in the moment that it was spontaneous. Her eyes were large and full of fire.

"Baby, I want you to take of your shirt now, show me those

beautiful boobs. Touch them, I want to see them, they are making me so fucking hard right now, I can't even think straight anymore."

She removes her shirt, and a pair of the most amazing tits I've ever seen appear. She's a slim girl, but her tits are amazingly big, god bless Eastern European girls. She starts playing with her tits slowly, and pays special attention to the nipples. My dick was raging, and I start to jerk off.

"Mhm, oh, baby, I'm totally touching myself right now, you are so fucking sexy when you do that. Listen, if I was there, I'd start kissing those amazing tits right now. I'd kiss them at the sides first, and then slowly work my way up to the nipples. Then I'd proceed to kiss all of your tummy, all the way down towards your pussy, but I wouldn't go there yet.

I'd firmly grab your thighs and kiss them, and I'd look deep into your eyes as I'd kiss you passionately. I'd start to massage your pussy with my hands, and I'd hear your moaning. Your hips would start moving and you would grab my hard dick. You'd be soaking wet by now, just like you are right now in your bedroom."

I see how she smiles in a naughty way, a silent confirmation.

"Baby, I want you to start touching yourself right now, I'm pretty close to coming to be honest. Seeing you being so sexy and imagining all these things turns me on so much. Listen, if I was there, I'd take down your panties now, and I'd start to play with your pussy. I'd put in one finger first, slowly, so I could feel all the wetness.

Then, I'd push the finger in all the way, and then push in and in, and then out, in and out."

I was speaking in a very slow and in a deep voice. It's hard to evaluate yourself, but I think it was damn fucking sexy.

"Soon I'd add a second finger, in and out, in and out... I can almost feel the warmth of your pussy on my fingers. Can you imagine how good it would feel like if I put my hard dick in there?"

At this moment, I rebalance the camera so she can see me jerking off my raging boner. She starts biting her lips and massaging her pussy up and down, really fast.

"And then just when you wouldn't be able to take it anymore, I'd put my dick in you. Slowly, but I'd continue all the way in. You'd start moaning and then our rhythm would get faster and faster, until I'd be fucking you really hard and fast, and then very soon, we'd both come at the same time and then collapse one onto another in a bundle of arms and legs..."

I came so hard, it was crazy. I saw she came too, which was awesome. With naughty smiles on our faces we both agreed that what we had just done was awesome, and then we said goodbye for the time being.

I went back to video editing, and for some reason, it was much easier to focus.

Chapter Sixteen
SO, ARE YOU GOING TO THE UNI, BRO?

Zurich, October 2015

Zurich is the first city where we all got super high together. In this city we met cool people, we ran all the events, and we generally had a blast. Max pulled a hottie out of a day game session, but the most memorable event was definitely the high.

Zurich is a beautiful city. But also very expensive. The most expensive I've experienced, and that's including having been to New York, London, Miami, Oslo and others. For example, a haircut for a guy would cost you $70. A regular shitty Chinese food delivery would cost $30 per person. Even bananas cost over $4/kg in a shop. When I saw that, I thought to myself:

"Damn, I guess it's pasta and muesli time."

It was my first time staying in a student dormitory, awesome. This cool guy Ben offered to host me and took me to his place. I immediately felt at home; it wasn't that long ago that I was staying in my own student dormitory back in Ljubljana, Slovenia. The only difference was that theirs was amazing. Balconies, a sick common room with sofas and a PS4, a full spacious kitchen and, best of all, private rooms for everyone.

And if that comes as a surprise to the reader, yes, in Slovenia, and most other Easter European countries student accommodations are mostly shared rooms. Which kind of sucks. However, our universities are still mostly free of charge, no five or six figures tuition fees, etc, so screw you.

Anyway, staying there was awesome. I even showed my host how easy it was to talk to chicks on the campus, I got us invited to a common kitchen party on a different floor and even helped him number-close a girl he liked. I also quickly ended up in the room of a cute Asian girl, yet her friends started to knock on the door before any sexyness could happen. Oh man, if I were a student again I would bang so much my dick would fall off.

Anyway, on Wednesday evening, my host Ben and myself join Max and Vini in their Airbnb. First task for me that day, go to the store and buy healthy snacks.

Grocery runs were one of the tasks I would regularly get. For example, every Monday night or Tuesday afternoon, as time allowed, I'd get a big checklist of grocery shopping I'd do for Max. He was really big on clean eating, so the grocery run would end up with me dragging a backpack and a large, heavy bag of cottage cheese, fruits and vegetables, olive oil, avocados, and other healthy food to Max's.

And funny enough, Max would act as if the grocery runs were boring but necessary, and was almost apologizing that I had to do them for him as his assistant.

But the thing is, I didn't mind, I liked grocery runs. I was discovering the new city, I got inspired and awe-struck. Later on, in the midst of tiredness that bordered on depression, a new city would still inspire me. I got some time to reflect, think, and just let my mind wonder, hell, I even got some number-closes along the way.

Anyway, back to Zurich's grocery run. That was the biggest pile of nuts, dark chocolate, and dried tropical fruits you've ever seen. And the most expensive too. I think I paid like $100 for a bag of healthy snacks. It was crazy, I'd never had such a healthy high before, usually stoners stuff their faces full of the worst junk food they can find.

Then I roll a joint, because no one else was any good at it. I'd always roll when we smoked, I guess I have some high-school weed history, haha. And then we smoke.

Damn, that weed was super strong, some Swiss Skunk right there. And for some reason we had five grams, even though none of us were hardcore smokers. One gram would have been more than enough for all of us, but I guess Ben wanted to outdo himself.

As usual, everything becomes super funny and we laugh like crazy. Max takes the HD projector we use for Free Tours and Hot Seats and plays the new Star Wars trailer in full HD on the wall. We are all mind fucked, it's such an awesome trailer. It's fun to travel with all this gear.

I'm so full of nuts and dark chocolate that I can barely move. We just troll and bullshit around for a while and then we do what people do at every good smoking party. We smoke the next joint. More laughing and good times follow.

It really was just an amazing moment, a great atmosphere. Being around Max and Vini was awesome. We were doing cool shit: traveling, meeting girls, and hustling hard, learning new stuff, discovering. If weed just intensifies your emotions, it totally dawned on us that evening that this is an amazing moment in our lives. I was really, really happy.

At some point I notice that Max had a good content idea for 'The Natural' (his future best-seller-to-be online course) and he immediately takes out his phone and records a voice note. Even while being high. That was another one of those things that I picked up, one of those little reasons why he is as successful as he is. No matter what happens, the hustle has an important role.

You see, I don't know if you've ever been high before, but when you are, you usually feel really lazy. And while being high, people usually get good ideas, it opens up the box of your mind a bit. But usually it just stays at the idea stage, because you forget it in the next 10 seconds. Well, not Max. He recorded the idea and then later created a Youtube video on the topic.

Then the pinnacle of the evening comes, a joke that never gets old between Max, Vini, and myself. Even to this day.

We notice Ben fell asleep. Ah damn. We need like five

minutes and a glass of water to wake him up. It's about 2am at this point. Then he slowly stands up and says he needs to go, as he has to wake up early the next day. I ask him:

"So, are you going to the Uni, bro?"

And then for some reason, Max, Vini and I start to laugh uncontrollably. Seriously, we laughed so hard I started to cry and Vini started to choke. And it lasted for a few minutes too. Ben was probably thinking something along the lines of: *"What the fuck?"* Before Ben left, we thanked him for his company and I told him I would return to his place in the morning.

You see, the big laugh was probably about all our crew despising the "normal life." Having to wake up early to go to uni, or work. We all had big plans and ambitions, and wanted to take over the whole world. We wanted to be the best, the greatest. Get the hottest girls, get masses of money, live big. Travel places, do things on our own terms.

And having a nine-to-five was definitely not a part of the plan. I'm not saying that having a nine-to-five is necessarily a bad thing, but we despised the thought of it. That's probably why the laugh was so powerful and also why we remember it so vividly.

And now anytime that somebody says *"So, are you going to the Uni, bro?"*, a smile creeps across our faces. If someone ever meets any one of us and pops that question, the reaction is always the same.

After that, we visited a local bakery. Max paid. He always paid for stuff like that. Call it team building, or what you like, but I think it was super cool. He didn't have to, but it made it much easier for Vini and I. Because even if I bought the baked goods myself, I'd feel guilty about going over my weekly budget. I guess Vini was even more stretched, he had been on tour for a year already and was from Brazil, which is not exactly the world's richest country.

So Max bought us a shitload of croissants, donuts, pizzas, and pies. So much for the healthy snacks. Stuffed ourselves full and fell asleep around 5am. I had the beautiful company of the floor, since Vini had the couch, and I couldn't be bothered to travel to my host's place.

I realized that it was actually the first time I had slept on the floor during this tour, and even that wouldn't have happened if I would have joined Ben and gone back to his place earlier.
Not bad at all!

Chapter Seventeen
PANTS DOWN CRAZE

Zurich, October 2015

We were becoming quite a crew. Team RSD Max in the house. One of the most epic nights of the whole adventure was definitely the last night of the Bootcamp in Zurich.

It's was a Saturday night. As usual we all roll into a club. Except it wasn't a club, but more of a giant youth centre. There was this big university party going down and we figured it would be the perfect place for our Bootcamp students, who were all in their early twenties this time.

See, at that time, I was 23. I just have a special feeling in my heart for student parties. They remind me of the good times during my exchange studies in Lithuania and my student days in Ljubljana, Slovenia. Plus, student girls are almost always amazing, I love them.

During the previous two days, we had been visiting some

more student parties. With all these young, fit and athletic, adventure-and-fun-seeking girls around me, I had been getting super horny. And I hadn't been able to do anything at all about it; I had been stuck filming somebody else having all the fun with these girls. Damn.

So we enter the club and the guys start pimping. By now I'm doing a pretty sick job with the camera too. Max talks to the students and sends them into sets. He and Vini do a few sets of their own. And, slowly but surely, the party vibe starts to hit us.

It's a funny phenomenon because none of us ever drinks, but the energy of the place and the people around kind of spills over. So you actually get the best out of it, you become louder, more expressive, less awkward, and social barriers fall. However, because you are sober, you can still think clearly and your motor skills are unfettered. Sweet!

At some point, we could all catch a few breaths since all the students were happily in sets. Then Vini somehow finds a small football. He and Max start to play football in the crowd and I join in as well. It was pure mayhem, colored lights flashing around, loud music banging, and me running after the two guys who are playing football in a night club, with a huge camera in my hands.

And then the DJ plays a Linkin Park song. Max goes completely crazy. He starts to head bang like only a true metalhead can. And if that's not enough, to my surprise, he takes off his shirt and drops his pants and does a sort of a manic dance in his underwear. Vini joins in and everyone around us goes crazy, they love it.

I am laughing my ass off now and film them completely openly, not giving much of a damn about anyone catching me. I stand in the open, even move around the guys to get circling shots and the like. I'm getting some amazing shots in. Soon the bouncer comes to check out what's up. He signals to the guys to put their pants back on. But they more or less ignore the security guy, who looks very helpless at this time.

See the thing is, the Swiss people are all about human rights and this was just some big student party, which probably wasn't even registered with the authorities or anything like that. So they didn't really want to use force to "kick us out." As a result I got an amazing shot of the guys dancing in their boxer shorts, with the bouncer standing only three meters away, with a confused look on his face not knowing what the hell to do.

He spots my camera too, but I just told him I was taking pictures. He doesn't really believe it, but he doesn't question it any further. He must have hated his part-time job at that moment. The song ends, the guys pull up their pants, and we figure it's best if we don't push our luck, and just move to one of the other areas, to give the poor bouncer a break.

Now, as I mentioned, I was really horny that night and I was also getting cocky. For example, shooting an infield video of Max with one hand and half of my attention, and talking to some girl at the same time. Remember, the filming itself is a piece of art, manually changing the settings according to the light levels, and the difficult focusing positions. Not really something you can do "off the cuff."

As you can imagine, I didn't catch all the shots that night, and I could see that Max wasn't very happy. And then I fucked up big time.

Max talks to some girl and she's loving it. It still surprised me, it was out of this world. This short, bearded, Austrian dude, talking to these absolute hotties, and them loving him. They would look deep inside his eyes, they'd ask him to take down their number, they have their hands all over him. I was well adjusted to it by then, but it still struck me from time to time.

As said, I was trying to game myself at the same time too. At some point he grabs the girl, lifts her over his shoulder and starts to run up the stairs with her. She is giggling like crazy and loving it. I ditched my girl and run after them with the camera, I knew something amazing could happen and I also knew that I had already missed a part of the epic shot.

Oh, I forgot to mention that Max was still shirtless at this time, this happened soon after the Linkin Park dance. Now, as I was following them, one of the bouncers was following me. Just imagine this scene for a moment.

A shirtless guy carrying a hot girl (who is giggling uncontrollably) in the direction of the toilets. And a guy with headphones and a camera blatantly filming and following them... Plus a bouncer in hot pursuit only a few steps behind.

Max carried the girl towards the toilets and then he kissed her. I was afraid of the bouncer following me, so I was wary and took more time to follow than usual. Once my camera popped into the angle to see the couple, I was a few moments too late and they had stopped kissing and the girl wanted to go back, starting to feel uncomfortable by the amount of people suddenly there.

We changed places again because of the bouncer (man, bouncers there were the worst, haha). And then we continued our night. More epic moments happened, and the students couldn't thank us enough for the epic Bootcamp they had.

One of them was approaching hot girls he had been intimidated of just days before. Another one pulled 2 girls to another friend's hotel room. All of them had a lot of fun, and a complete shift of their mindset. Talking to girls was not something scary or a chore anymore. It became a skill, that can bring amazing people in your life, as long as you put in some work and some balls.

Flash forward to the next afternoon, Max asks me about my filming the previous night. He checks the footage and then gets upset.

"What the fuck man, how could you miss that, you know how much a shot like this matters? I might never be in a mood like this again, it was totally epic. Plus the girl was totally down and super hot. You know how much my brand could grow with some shots like this? It's not a joke, man, the value here was real. It could show the guys that there's nothing wrong with relaxing and letting go, in fact, it can be attractive if you truly own it.

You joined this team to film, not game, and we both agreed that would be your priority. I just want you to know that you completely fucked up and that your mistake will cost me a lot.

Just saying."

He was more disappointed than angry, and that hurt. I saw him as a mentor, as a boss, and to be honest, we had become good friends too. And I realized I had fucked up. So I apologized and proposed a solution.

"Yeah man, I'm sorry. You're right, I wasn't doing my job properly. And yes, the shot would be fucking sick, none of the other instructors has anything like that. I just... you know, wanted to game too. I'm super horny and I love student parties like this and I just wanted to get a girl too."

Max gave me a strangely understanding "been there done that" look, and said:

"Well, you know what, talk to Vini. Maybe he can take your turn filming one night a week or something like that, and you can help him with the coaching and game yourself a little bit too."

And that was that. I had admitted my mistake, I felt really bad about it, but had also gotten one film-free night a week. I guess Max understood I was just human too, and what united us in the first place was the passion for the game, and I think he could feel that. I really, really appreciated it and Max's worth grew yet again in my eyes.

It was one of those things that just increased my respect for him as time passed. If you faced Max with a fact, he'd evaluate it and then act accordingly. Even if the fact was painful, or difficult to accept, he'd always consider it and act accordingly.

Chapter Eighteen
A CONSTANT IN MY LIFE

London, October 2015

We flew to London after Zurich. Immediately after entering the tube station from the airport, I felt at home.

The Oyster recharge machines, busy people sprinting up and down the tube station, the dirty, fast food chicken shops, all the mixed accents and colors. London is pretty cool. And I had lived there for about a year before joining Max.

We had to reach Shoreditch, a super hipster area with lots of bars, clubs, graffiti, weed and, well, hipsters. Our host was a super cool guy with a funny French accent. This was only the second time that all three of us had crashed at the same place. Max had a room of his own, Vini had the couch, and I grabbed the floor mat.

Ah well.

I was getting really excited too, because Alex lived in London. So straight after we arrived, I headed out to buy the groceries for Max (in a familiar Sainsbury's supermarket) and then jumped on one of those big red double-decker buses and headed towards Upper Holloway, North London. It was close to 9pm and I was excited as hell.

The situation was quite funny at the time. Alex and I really liked each other, we had only seen each other two times, but we had been writing to each other every few days, and we had had Skype sex about two weeks ago. This was gonna be interesting.

I definitely wanted to have sex with her. She was super hot: 19 years old, tight athletic body, long curly brown hair. And she was really cool too. She's the type of girl you can take hiking, and she's a girl who wouldn't be afraid of getting dirty if you were working on the house. And at the same time she's super feminine too, knows how to look good and be seductive too. Great combination.

However, the one obstacle that can prevent you getting laid often, even if you have good game and/or connection, is logistics; in this case, simply a place private enough where I could get down to business. Luckily for me, I have a lot of friends and people I know in London, so I asked my buddy Theodore to lend me his room. He was living super close to her anyway.

I met her in the park close to Theodore's house, the park where we had initially met. And where we would continue to meet regularly afterwards; it's a cute little park. I walk to the meeting spot, about 10 minutes late as always. I actually am slightly nervous, but I learned not to show it. I see her in the distance, waiting for me. It's dark already, it's about 9pm.

The first few seconds of the date with someone who you haven't seen for a while are always a little bit awkward, but I know this feeling now, so I plough through. Throw in a big smile, hug her, take her under the arm and start walking. Start chatting about regular stuff like travel and how we have both been doing in the recent weeks. And of course throw in some teasing too.

We first walk to the shop, to buy some food. Risotto was the plan. Risotto is always the plan when I first invite a girl home to cook. It's super easy, quick, and tastes amazing. So we buy the food and head straight to Theodore's place.

The cooking is a lot of fun, there is some sexual tension already, but she's laid back about it. I don't mind, because it's better when the seduction process is slower. It's kind of like just munching down a whole bar of dark chocolate versus savoring it piece by piece.

Once or twice in between, I step close to her, start breathing on her neck and touch her hips. I lean in as if to kiss her, but then back away at the last moment. I see the sparks in her eyes; she is getting turned on, and so am I.

We eat the risotto. It tastes pretty good, as always. I don't eat too much (I normally eat huge amounts of food) because I don't want to have my stomach full. I know I'll eat again afterwards.

Then I take her straight to the room, we both knew why we met, I mean, after that Skype in Berlin, all I could think of is how hot her ass and tits were.

I put on some music and start kissing her straight away. She's such a good kisser, very passionate, but allows me to lead. Things get really hot, really fast. We are passionately kissing, clothes are flying off, and very soon I find myself putting a condom on.

I did all the things I told her I will in the Skype call.

I started off kissing her body, touching her everywhere until she became really loud and I could feep her hands grasping me and clawing my back. After she was really wet, and I finger her. First with one finger, and then with two, while stimulating her clitoris with the other hand.

Just as she started to moan in a really sexy way, I slowly entered her. The sex was pretty good; not amazing, but certainly not bad. It's never as good with a new person as with somebody you are more used to.

Funny enough, I was slightly afraid of my friend the limp dick, but there was no sign of him here. She was just so hot, and I was super comfortable.

After that we lie in the bed for some time, cuddle and talk. I feel super relaxed, this is the time off that I need, it feels really good. No editing, no trying to prove myself, no filming. No running around like a headless chicken, no lifting weights. Just lying in the bed, with this awesome hot girl next to me, thinking of nothing.

Just enjoying the moment, and feeling her body's heat next to me.

After 15 minutes or so we both get horny again, so we fuck again. This time we don't use a condom (she's on the pills) and it's even better. It wasn't as gentle and passionate as before: this one was pure, hardcore fucking.

Biting, scratching, and sweating. I remember pulling her hair as I was behind her doggy style, my pelvis pushing against her perfect ass, while her moans are telling me she's enjoying it as much as I am.

At some point I had to put my fingers in her mouth because I was afraid that Theodore's flatmates will give us some shit because of how loud we were. Makes me hard just thinking about it. My balls bouncing off her perfect ass, while I'm pulling her hair with one hand and letting her suck the fingers of the other while I fuck her. I come inside of her very soon, and then we just lie there together, both breathing heavily in a state of pure ecstasy.

A few months later on, she would tell me that she doesn't like the romantic thing that much, how she loves it when I fuck her hard and aggressive. Most girls actually prefer that, at least to my knowledge. Not always, and not all girls, but it's good to talk about these sorts of things.

We continue to lie in the bed for some time, cuddle and chat some more. It's getting late and I had heard Theodore fall asleep on the sofa in the common room. We get dressed, wake Theodore up, thank him, and leave. I escort her home, passionately kiss her goodbye, and tell her I'll try to meet her later on in the week.

Chapter Nineteen
A FIGHT WITH MY DAD

London, October 2015

The following week was very busy.

London was hardcore, a Free Tour with over 400 people, a full Bootcamp, and then the biggest paid RSD live event ever: over 100 guys attending the Max Hot Seat. Max, Vini, and I all worked our balls off the entire week.

And it's not like the dragging commuting time in London helped. However, we were comfortable putting in all we had, because a week off, a full week with no programs, was just around the corner.

My plan was to have an extra three days in London, and then fly to Sofia, Bulgaria a few days ahead of Max and Vini, so I could relax a little and game for myself a bit. It was getting harder to just film all the time. I wanted to pimp it on my own too.

At some point I remember meeting my dad at my host's place. My dad had just moved to London a few weeks ago - and I had helped him find a season job in an outdoor sports equipment shop. That's a pretty cool thing to do to be honest: a dude over 50 moving out of his country just like that.

Not bad!

We have some food and a chat, we talk about everything. I explain to him exactly what I am doing for Max. He's a bit of a skeptical about the whole "teaching guys how to get laid" thing, but he is pretty much cool and open about it, which is really good.

However, when the conversation reaches the subject of my pay, and he realizes I am not only doing all this for free, but also burning a lot of my own money along the way, he gets a bit frustrated.

"He's using you. What are you thinking? All that money you worked so hard to get, you're spending it to do work for someone else, for free!?"

And that's when I got pissed off.

I'm interesting when I get pissed off. I am very direct, and speak with a strong, sharp voice, but I don't shout. I look the person straight in the eye, and don't let them speak until I am finished. There's this icy feeling to it, it's hard to describe. I feel powerful and almost invincible, yet it's tough to control the feeling.

It doesn't happen often, maybe once or twice a month. I have a very strong urge for self-preservation, and when someone attacks my work or beliefs, especially someone very close to me, I protect myself. I had been forced to learn not to let people walk all over me.

"Oh, yeah? Thanks for advice, dad. However, if I remember correctly, I've been supporting myself ever since I moved out at 19. If I remember correctly, it was me who helped you find a job because you couldn't find anything worthwhile yourself? So please, have a little faith in me, and keep advice like that to yourself."

I attacked his weakest point. It stung him, and I could see he was hurt. Obviously it's not easy for a grown man to face the fact that he's financially worse off than his son. But he took it well, sucked it up, and apologized. I was a bit sorry as well, so I went on, and tried to explain my view on the thing.

"The fact is, yes, I am working for free, but I am also learning awesome skills. For example, I know how to use a professional camera now, I know what kind of shots are good, I know how to use microphones and other filming gear. I'm getting good at editing videos too. Those are really valuable skills.

In addition, I'm learning great branding and marketing skills. I'm learning how social media, especially Youtube and Facebook work, how to create quality content. I'm networking with successful people all over the world. Not to mention, I will have travelled most of the Europe and a part of the USA by the end of this tour. That's nothing to be laughed at."

I see understanding in his eyes and am a bit sorry I came out so hard. But if I had another chance, I'd repeat it. Succeeding and dreaming big is hard enough as it is, and if people close to you offer doubt instead of their 100% support, well, they're not helping much, are they?

Obviously, honest advice is one thing, but mindless preaching is quite another.

The mood soon turns from tense, to less tense, to more chill. One of the things that I share with my dad is the love for cooking, and the meal was awesome. We had pasta with minced meat sauce. Included was lot of onions, tomato sauce, and a big pile of vegetables, all sprinkled with freshly grated parmesan cheese... Oh my god, that was awesome.

I stuff my face full of food and then chat with my dad about his plans in London. We talk about my siblings, about mom (my parents are divorced), about life back in Slovenia. It's good to catch up, and a nice, and warm feeling slowly creeps into me.

It doesn't last long though, the hustling is calling, and as much fun as catching up is, it gets boring fast. Sometimes I think my ambition will consume me, haha. They say that the candle that burns twice as bright, burns half as long...

I say goodbye to my dad, and then continue the hustle.

Chapter Twenty
THE TEMPTATION
OF THE DARK SIDE

London, Halloween 2015

Saturday was a crazy day.

It was Halloween, so Vini and I decided to go out and pimp even though we were fucking tired.

It was after 1am when we had finished our work for the day and arrived home. Max was already teaching Bootcamp.

We needed to get some testimonials on tape and tidy the seminar room, as usual. Cabbing it back took some time, since London traffic was a mess - and even more so, because it was Halloween. So we were't exactly in a party mode to begin with.

I know how us game guys are all healthy and don't drink etc, but we have a few shots each despite that. Vini decides on vodka and I had some whiskey – cheers to our lovely host's welcoming mini-bar. That actually gives us a bit of energy, and we head to catch the bus towards central London. It's 1.30am at this point.

At the bus stop, Vini and I just chill and troll. We talk to some musician guy and then I make Vini go talk to some cute vampire girl, even though he didn't want to at first. Her bus shows up about 5min later. And then to my absolute surprise, Vini ventures onto the bus with her.

My mind was blown. I wasn't sure how it'll end up for him, but I knew it would make no sense for me to wait for him, so I just send him some thumbs up emojis and boarded a central-bound bus myself; my plan was to meet Max there after his Bootcamp.

I chat up some cute Russian girl on the bus. We have a bit of a banter and it's going well, I like her smile. She wouldn't come with me no matter what I said, but she gave me her black swan wings, which I totally abused to get other girls to open me. It was 3am by the time I met up with Max, thanks to London's "amazing" traffic. We were both super tired, so we decided to just Uber it back home.

In the meantime, we receive a text from Vini, about 2 hours after I last saw him:

"She's so nice, she's making me toast after some awesome sexyness."

After the text there's a pic of the hot vampire chick, only from waist down in the kitchen. She had really hot legs and ass. Me and Max are totally happy and excited for Vini, and send him some cheeky texts.

On the way back, Max opens three girls who are sitting on the floor. All the usual: chit chat, some jokes, and the girls open up and chat to us. But at some point Max starts to banter with one of the girls with a bit more negativity than normal.

"I understand, you are too drunk to converse properly. That's cool. Oh, maybe you should treat your boyfriend better and he wouldn't cheat on you... You're getting a little bigger too. Have you stopped exercising recently...?"

The girl became super defensive and mean in return.

"Yeah, why did you even start talking to us you fucking cunt? My problems with my boyfriend are none of your problems, get lost. By the way, your outfit doesn't look like Darth Vader at all, it looks like a retarded bat. Go to hell."

And to be honest, I kind of understood her. Max was actually being a dick. That was some really dark shit, I have never seen him being negative to a girl before. I asked him about it, and he explained that some girls, usually the ones with low self-esteem, actually respond to negativity better.

Because that's what they are used to. A lot of the very hot girls are actually very self-conscious, so hitting on their insecurities works well.

It made sense, so I asked no further. Yet I could sense he was not at his best and there was something bugging him. Couldn't say exactly what it was though.

When I asked him about the event after the whole tour was over, he expanded on the topic:

"Yeah, the negativity works, but it is also massively 'low vibration.' You probably don't even want girls like that in your life; that was not the best practice by me at the time. I don't do shit like that anymore."

I've seen Max perform similar verbal spikes on a few more occasions after that event, and I can confirm that it didn't come from a good place. Either he was in a bad mood, tired, or really wanted to close the girl, or something slightly evil broke out that was a combination of various factors. Those spikes seemed to work, but I didn't like them one bit.

That was my starting lesson of negativity in game, and it might sound funny but it reminded me of Star Wars, where Master Yoda would say:

"Powerful you have become, dark side I sense in you."

After some reflection and talking to Vini, it struck me how extreme the game can be.

On one hand, a guy can meet a girl on a bus stop, leave with her to her home, and then have sex with her and get some toast on top of that.

And on the other hand, it can make you mindfully provoke negative emotions in a girl simply to make her attracted to you.

The rabbit hole indeed ran deep...

Chapter Twenty-One
THE FIRST
HONEYMOON
PERIOD

London, November 2015

Sunday evening came. We were finally done with work, and Max invited Vini and I, together with the guys who had done testimonials for us, to watch Ridley Scott's "*The Martian.*" As awesome an offer as that is, I decided to decline and meet up with Alex instead.

When I parted with Max and Vini for the week, I got to keep the AV bag, which contained a lot of different electronic bullshit. On top of all the wires and gadgets, there was also our super sweet HD projector that we used for Free Tour and the Hot Seat seminars. So my date idea for Sunday was pretty easy, movie night in my room.

My room? But didn't I say I was crashing on the floor in London? Yes I was, but since Max was leaving the next day, our lovely French host agreed for me to stay on in Max's room for the extra three days. And for that night, Max didn't mind me using the room till they are back. Awesome!

It was just perfect. Lying in the bed with my girl, watching "*Step Up 3*", feeling the warmth of her body, the shape of her ass. I really wanted to see the full movie because I hadn't seen it in ages. I know it's corny and all that, but I still like it. However, I think I lasted about 30min and then started to kiss her everywhere. She didn't mind at all, she returned my passion equally, if not even more.

What can I say, those three days were so amazing. I met my girl twice and most of the time we would just have sex. I'm not just saying that, I mean it. Like we'd literally have sex 3 or 4 times in the course of a few hours spent together. Even after I was super tired and my dick would hurt, I'd somehow still get horny around her. She was just so hot, she had an amazing sexual vibe, I could not get enough of her.

I still remember the times vividly: the two of us, just lying there in the bed after sex, my hands gliding over her naked body in the dim light. Deep vocal house music playing in the back, no thoughts in my head, just presence, and sharing. Two young lovers, both far away from their home, seeking their place in the world and sharing the intensity of emotions with one another.

The sex was getting better and better too; we couldn't get enough of each other. I mean, obviously it would be difficult to go wrong here. She was a super hot and chilled-out 19-year old, bored of her babysitting job, and I was a young dude, full of hormones and energy, who was traveling the world trying to learn how to get laid better.

I had gotten laid a few times since starting the tour, but those times were just one-night stands. One-night stands are cool, but, by definition, you actually don't get to have regular sex that much. You need to get to know a partner first to please them better, and vice versa.

Besides pure fucking, I got increasingly attached to her too.

She was sweet. We talked about about things: what I wanted to do in life, what she wanted to do in hers. We talked about our friends, our families back at home, passions, fears. And she was always so cool; I could totally relax and be myself with her.

One of the things I appreciated the most when spending time with her, even later on, is that she would never be jealous or try to pick a fight. She'd let me do my stuff, and once I came back to her she would appreciate the time she had with me. And that's why I always gave all I had to her. All my passion, all my loving, all my care.

We made cool pictures, we'd cook, I'd escort her home, we'd draw funny drawings, we'd tease each other. All sorts of innocent things like that. And then when I was touring we would just continue to text and Skype. She'd proceed to become my queen. But not just yet. Some dark shit needed to happen before that.

I remember how I escorted her to her bus the last night before my flight to Sofia. It was a Tuesday night, around 1am. Not many people were around at the time, and it was getting chilly. We walked, hand-in-hand, and just casually talked. But there was something pressing both of us, I'd leave soon and not come around again for god knows how long.

We reached the bus stop, and kind of stopped talking. We still had about 10min before the bus came. I didn't like the atmosphere, the words stopped flowing, and a sad silence began.

So I repositioned myself from sitting at her side, to actually sitting on her, facing her, basically mounting her. I figured that I don't want to leave a sad impression, something sexy would work better. We then passionately kissed and hugged for those 10 minutes and it was awesome.

Alex boarded the bus, and I waved goodbye. I then left without looking back.

I always left her without looking back, because looking back would be really difficult.

Chapter Twenty-Two
£100 CAR RIDE

London, November 2015

So on the day of the flight from London, two of my buddies escort me to the tube station. We left early enough and had plenty of time. We take pictures before I say goodbye, I catch the tube, enter Liverpool Street station and check where my train is. Sweet, the train is called Stansted Express, and is leaving for Stansted airport in ten minutes. Awesome!

I jump on the train, sleep on the way there, and then casually drag my suitcase to flight info boards. And then I realize I can't find the bag drop area. I was flying with Wizz Air, some low-cost Hungarian air carrier. I was searching for their pink colors, but they were nowhere to be found. I ask some security guards, they're unsure where it is.

And then I realize it. I'm supposed to fly out from Luton, but I'm at Stansted.

"Fuck!"

I start sweating like hell, and start thinking about logistics with full speed. So I have approximately two hours before take-off, and I am at the wrong airport. Bag drop-in closes forty minutes before the flight, so I have exactly one hour and twenty minutes to get there.

"Fuck!"

I run towards the taxi stands. Stansted airport is huge. It takes me a few minutes of jogging, and by the time I get there I'm drenched in sweat. I speak to the lady there:

"How much for a taxi to Luton Airport?"

"About 100 pounds, sir."

"Fuck, FUCK!"

"How long does it take to get there?"

"Well, about one hour and fifteen minutes, sir. But it really depends on the traffic."

"AAAAAA, FUCK!"

I think for two seconds and then I pass her my credit card. *Fuck it, let's go!* I follow my driver out and to his car. Fortunately, it's close. We get in, my heart is beating really fast. I know I have to explain the situation to him, so he will drive faster. However, if I just try to boss him around, he will hate me. I was very socially savvy even before the tour, but that just increased when working for Max.

"So, how's your day today, is there a lot of work?"

I chit-chat with him for a minute or two. I think I even manage to bust out a joke. And then I tell him the situation. He's a very cool guy, he says he'll do his best. I feel the car accelerating. I lean back, take a deep breath and close my eyes. I've done what I could.

I let go and start to meditate. It's very hard to focus, but better than thinking "what if?" and frustrating myself even further.

I check Google Maps every three minutes or so. Every time that I do that, I get the same answer. Google calculates that I will be late by a few minutes and it will be a near miss.

However, Google did not know that my driver was an absolute boss. And as far as he was concerned, I was not going to miss my flight. I prayed there would be no delays or accidents on the road.

In my mind, I had already envisioned option B: spending the night at the Luton airport. Now, I've slept at airports plenty of times and have always been fine with it. But on those occasions I already had a ticket for the following day, last minute tickets can be expensive.

"Fuck."

Also in the back of my mind, as you might remember, was the fact that I wasn't even getting paid. A new flight ticket might cost the same as a week or two of traveling. It's a shitty feeling, when you're doing something awesome, but know that you might have to stop doing that rather soon, because of financial issues.

I still had about half of my savings, but they were starting to run out. And losing about 250 pounds just because I didn't check which airport I fly from seemed very harsh.

My driver is such a boss that we arrive at Luton airport at 9:17pm, with the bag drop-off finishing at 9.20pm. So I jump out of car, grab both of the big bags: I had the AV and my big blue bag, plus my backpack. One bag on wheels in each hand, I start running as quickly as I can. I was pretty fast to be honest.

When I get to the main door, which is about a five minute walk from the car park (I ran it in two minutes), I still had some distance to go. Yet, I only have one more minute and I can't run anymore. I am sweaty, mad tired, and out of breath. I half-run and half-limp my way to the bag drop-off. I was four minutes too late.

The young guy at the desk asks me:

"Where to?"

"Sofia."

He checks the computer. His eyes grow big.

"Oh shit man, you're late."

"I know, is there anything you can do?"

He rings the control center and speaks to them. I can hear them saying "no" to him the first time, but then he asks them again. Eventually they decide to let my bag through. The guy gives me my ticket and tells me to go to through the security quickly. I thank him, and then fall into bliss. I start breathing again, I notice I am drenched in sweat, but, at the same time am, so, so happy.

I make my way through the security and on the way take a very expressive selfie, coupled with a motivating and honest text about my experience and post that shit to Facebook. The post gets more than 100 likes and a lot of comments, which is a pretty good number for my circle of friends. Here's the post, raw and uncut:

"Arrive at Stansted airport at 19.05. Realize I fly from Luton, at 21:10. Run to the taxi stand, how much? £100. Fuck, swipe the card, run to taxi (w two suitcases). Stressed as fuck, calmly explain situation to driver, he speeds up. It's 60 mins to there, baggage drop closes in 55. I meditate on the way. We come to Luton at 20.03, well done driver, but, he can't park close to the gate. I give him £5 (which I luckily had in my pocket cause my buddy returned it to me). He drives into car park, close to gate, I sprint out of taxi. 20.08 enter Luton, run to baggage, there exactly when they close, 20.10. They make a phone call, let me in. I get the biggest grin and start breathing again.

When you are on your mission, the universe gets out of the way. Booyah! :D c u in Sofia!"

— at London Luton Departures.

Chapter Twenty-Three
SOFIA, EASTERN EUROPEAN GIRLS & MY HOSTS

Sofia, November 2015

I arrived at Sofia a few days before we started working, so I was feeling extremely happy. Recharged from a few days with my Czech girl and ready for new adventures.

I step out of the airplane and a funny thing happens, I see a girl eyeballing me. I get that now sometimes, but there was more of it there. Some girl on the bus transfer even says *"Welcome to Sofia."* It's super unusual, but I like it. Oh and also, the girls seem very hot.

So on my way to the baggage claim, I see this hot girl. Obviously I chat her up: *"Are you from Sofia?"* We talk for a bit, get our bags, and proceed to the exit. I seize the moment and ask her to get a quick drink with me. She agrees, and we go to some airport cafe.

Oh btw, the airport was SUPER run down. This Soviet-style building, with weird Cyrillic letters that I couldn't read. Intimidating guys, tall, muscular, and mostly without hair. Everything looked kinda alien. But then again, I was chilling with a Bulgarian girl, and she seemed to know her stuff, I didn't really feel afraid or anything like that.

Anyway, we order our drinks and, to my surprise, she INSISTS on paying for both. That never happens. I mean, both drinks and the chewing gums for me were like 2€ or something, super cheap, but still, dude, what the hell? Sofia is obviously gonna be awesome!

We finish the drink, she helps me find a cab, and tells me the rough price in order to not get ripped off. I number-close her and let her go. She's going to a different city, so I probably won't see her again, but you never know.

I meet my host late at night. Again I'm crashing at some student dorm a bit out of the center. I have my own bed, so I'm a happy panda.

Now let's say a few words about my hosts. Well, my hosts are all guys who I found online via Facebook, guys who support RSD. I introduced myself as RSD Max's assistant, and that implied I know a lot about game. They were always really happy to host me, because they knew they would get their share of the value. And they always did – I'm still good friends with some of my hosts.

Sometimes, I'd get my own room with a host, though rarely. Usually, it was a couch in the living room, or an extra mattress on the floor. Sometimes, I think two or three times on the whole tour, I'd crash on the floor. That wasn't super nice, but wasn't too bad either. And boy, did I meet a lot of people and see a lot of cool places like that.

I've stayed in everything from a penthouse suite in Copenhagen to crashing on a floor mat in London. I've gotten a free room in Miami Beach, and a student dorm room in Zurich. Really awesome places, and even more awesome hosts. I even pulled with some of my hosts, and some hosts (I'm sorry) were forced to listen me bang chicks while I was in the same room.

Anyway, next day I chill and walk around with my host. Do some day game in the centre, girls are super hot and really easy to chat up. I buy a strip rope bag I always wanted to have in some outlet store. It cost me €5, I was pretty happy about that. For the first time in my life I was rich. I mean not really, but in comparison to most people there, I was pretty damn well off.

My host has something to do later on, so I continue to explore the city on my own. I was waiting for the bus back home and it took forever. I had no idea what the hell is going on, but I was in a great mood. Discovering a new place always puts me in a great mood.

I open a group of girls and ask them what's up with the bus. They are also not sure, they are a bunch of new students in town. But regardless, we start to chat and vibe, crack jokes, etc.

Bus finally comes, I think after twenty minutes, instead of five, and we go to the same direction. It's just so awesome, they all love me. Before getting off, we make plans to party together, I Facebook-close the hottest girl of the group and continue to go home.

Later on, I ring my mum. It has been about two weeks

since we have last been in touch. A pretty regular and comfortable time frame. She was happy for me, she said she was in Sofia once too. I enjoyed talking to her, and had a big smile on my face after.

Next day is similar. The first difference from the day before was that I found a beautiful athletics stadium and did a kick ass workout there in the morning. The weather was still very warm there, despite it being early November. I even managed to attempt to do some shirtless sun tanning, it was that warm.

I say attempt, because I'm so pale I never get really tanned, all I get is freckles if I'm lucky, and sunburn if I'm not.

The second difference was that besides day gaming and discovering stuff, I was meeting the girl from the bus.

She is super hot. Skinny, great English, long straight brown hair, big eyes. I would imagine a girl like her when Inner Circle plays the song *"Sweat."*

"A La La La La Long Long.
Li Long Long Long.
I'm looking in your eye
I'm looking in your big brown eye.
(Ooh yeah)"

She has awesome feminine energy, which I started to notice quite a lot in Sofia. We go to this ghetto pizzeria for a drink, because the nice place next to it was closed (it was Sunday). By ghetto I mean everybody smoked inside, the staff didn't seem to care that much about us, and the place seemed, again, really run down and Soviet.

But no worries, circumstances don't matter. All the girl

really cares about is you. So we have a kickass time, we even draw some pictures with the crayons in the children's corner, chat, etc. There was a moment where I could kiss her, but decided not to.

If you show too much sexual intent early on, the girl might not be willing to come to your place soon after the date. And I definitely wanted to go for the pull. After an hour or so, I tell her I needed some groceries. We head towards the grocery shop, which is situated really near my place. Same story with the shop, it was super ghetto, haha.

We buy some groceries and then I lead her straight to my place. Obviously I texted my host to see if he can give me a spare hour or so. We come up, and she becomes super, super tense. I try to make her comfortable, but after five minutes or so she insists that she needs to go, so I agree with that and let her go. I'm a disappointed, but ah well.

And then my host comes with some bad news. His sister broke up with her boyfriend, because they had a fight and the boyfriend physically assaulted her. She was going to come to crash at my host's place, so he asked me to find another host asap.

I had some more offers from the Inner Circle Sofia guys from before, so I texted another guy who gladly took me in.

Chapter Twenty-Four
POKER PLAYERS & MAX'S OUTBURST

Sofia, November 2015

It's good that I had a few days off, because the short notice moving was somewhat stressful. However, the new host was super cool. A pro poker player. And his flatmate was actually a Bootcamp student, also a pro poker player.

Their crib was super awesome and we went out pimping the first night and had an awesome time together.

Next day Max and Vini arrived, and I met them at the airport later in the evening, to help them with the luggage and just to say "Hi." We haven't seen each other for a week, but I already missed those "assholes." Then I popped home to get my computer and was off to Max's again.

By the way, we would travel everywhere by taxi in Sofia. It was incredibly cheap. I mean, REALLY cheap. A 10min cab ride would cost you 2 or 3€, including the tip. That's another thing I noticed there. I love the feeling of having enough money to afford a taxi without killing my budget.

There, I made a promise to myself that I will get to the lifestyle that will allow me that anywhere in the world. Not spending like a retard, but being able to just take a cab and not worry about it. Or go eat out to some nice restaurant instead of some fast food crap and not worry. I wanted it as soon as possible. And I was dead serious.

It was getting late, and I found some weed, so that Max, Vini and I could have a nice night off. My host and his flatmate, the Bootcamp student, drive me towards Max's, and then ask if they can come too. To me, that was a completely normal question, plus they helped me find and buy the weed too. So we arrive at the door, and I let Max know that I'm there, plus that I have some extra people with me.

Then Max totally lost it.

I get a text:

"What the fuck man, what are you thinking? Just inviting people to smoke weed with us, seriously, are you fucking retarded? Plus, it's a Bootcamp student too, how do you think that will work? Dude seriously, I don't know, send them back or something, what the fuck man..."

Ok, I didn't expect that. I make up some excuses to the guys and apologize. I feel like shit for being such a dick to them. Also, I don't know what to expect from Max now, he seems really upset. They guys are obviously surprised and sad as well.

I feel pretty bad, to be honest. Max doesn't just lose it like that usually; even the time when I fucked up big time in Zurich he was more chill. It sucked. I guess he had a reason, he usually does, but I thought he was massively overreacting.

I come in the flat, say hi to Greg, Max's friend who'll be staying with Max and Vini for the week. Btw, he's a professional poker player too, making more money than Max, and just likes to travel and pimp, so he joins Max from time to time. I come in and face Max. He's still a bit pissed, but also sorry.

"Hey man. I mean, dude, what were you thinking, just invite everybody to Max's place, why not..."

I explain to him that I get it, and that I shouldn't invite anyone before specifically confirming with him.

"But you know Max, all that swearing and the "are you fucking retarded." that's not cool man. I didn't feel good when I read that. I mean, I work my ass off every day for you and seeing you act like that, that is not cool man."

His expression changed, he looked down for a second and then back to me. I can see he feels bad about it.

"Okay, I'm sorry man. I shouldn't have said those things, it's just, I got scared. I get really uneasy around new people, especially if we're gonna get high. I'll watch my words from now on, okay. But please, don't just invite people. I know you're super positive and think everybody is your friend, and I like this energy that you bring into the team, but I've been fucked over many times before, I'm just being wary."

I felt really good after talking about it and we had a really quality high.

I only learned why Max was uneasy about new people much later. There were some dark stories and adventures in his life. I guess everybody eats a lot of shit when they climb towards the top.

The next days, we proceed to do our shit as normal. Tuesday and Wednesday were project nights, lots of editing and hustling, and then we had the Bootcamp from the weekend onwards, along with the Free Tour and Hot Seat. Busy, busy times. And whenever I would pass by Max's place in Sofia, I would see a tattoo studio on the ground floor.

It was strangely alluring.

It was your typical tattoo place, just a little nicer. Pictures on the walls, big glass walls so you could see inside, everything seemed clean. Red neon sign saying "Tattoos." and even some writing in English, which was not common at all in Bulgaria.

I always admired tattoos, yet I had none. I love graffiti too. I'm a very visual guy, my eyes bring me a lot of beauty. So I had played with the thought of getting a tattoo many times before. But now the thought was stronger.

In addition, I was in the right state of mind. I finally understood that execution is key in life, not just planning. I knew nothing in life is permanent, and there was a very pragmatic reason too: the tattoo here would be MUCH cheaper. And, after all, I was on this crazy girl-chasing world tour too.

So one day I pop into the shop, just to inquire a little bit. I see this artistic soul type of guy there, drawing. I ask him a little bit about tattoos, how long do they last, could I get one on Sunday, can they do one of these pictures? He explains the process really well, and is super nice to me.

He was too nice to be a good seller, but I had pretty much set my mind already, so I pushed for the sale myself.

I agreed to come on Sunday.

Chapter Twenty-Five
ALWAYS DO ONE MORE

Lay Report, November 2015

Sofia Inner Circle Facebook Group

So it's a Tuesday, which is in most cities a pretty shit night to go out. I'm not feeling super good, because I had a few dates that led nowhere in the days before. Shitloads of contacts, but zero sex and not a lot of affection, etc. It's also been about a week since I saw my Alex in London, so I have started to get a little needy and very horny.

Anyway, some video editing work actually helped me to get into a better mood and then when my mind went retarded from staring at the screen at around 1am, I decided to go out with my host and his flatmate. Lately my self-amusement in game is skyrocketing, like NOTHING can bring my mood down, it's crazy.

#Self-Amusement

A principle in game. You should never be dependent on how you feel internally on external stimuli, meaning your friends, alcohol, music, or some girl's approval. You should find this in yourself. To make it more practical, an example is you talking about Borat jokes in the club, even though the other speaker might not consider them funny. But you do, and that's what matters. If they don't like that, they are free to leave, and you can find someone who will enjoy jokes like that.

So we shoot the shit in the car with my hosts, arrive at the first club, which was supposedly "The place to be on a Tuesday." We enter just after some pimp-ass Ferrari dudes. So funny, such a large gap between the rich and the poor here in Bulgaria. Anyway, no entrance fee, sweet. We get inside. Again, just fucking tables in the club.

I had gamed Thursday through Saturday last weekend, I had some off time, and most clubs in Sofia were like this. Big, very very loud, and a shitload of tables. People mostly just sit at their little table and hang out with friends, rarely do they talk to other people, or go dance and mingle. Maybe they will start moving and socializing at around 5am, just before closing, when they are shitfaced drunk. It was so unlike most places I've ever seen, and I've seen quite a lot.

So when you open the girls, there's a lot of social pressure. Even if they like you they are obliged to more or less politely tell you to fuck off, otherwise all their friends would judge them and think they're easy.

Anyway, no problem, I'm used to it now. First three sets I open are all classic hot "blasé" girl blowouts.

"Hi."

She turns her head slowly, looks at me, and then looks away. As if I'm not there.

"Is it because I'm from Slovenia?"

Big grin on my face. It does hurt a little, but mostly zero fucks given. I've learned how to handle this most of the time. This is the thing nobody talks about when talking about game, especially people who have never done it themselves.

It hurts like hell when you put yourself on the line, try to start a conversation with a girl you like, and she rejects you. When you start, it might happen 50 times in a night. It fucking sucks, I get it why some guys quit. But you grow immune to it sooner or later, you develop a thick skin.

Anyway, that's how the night goes. We hop to a few other clubs after that, and nothing really crazy happens. I get a few more contact details, we almost end up singing karaoke, and I help a buddy of mine number close a hot waitress. Fun times, but I'm getting tired, it's about 4.30am.

The guys want to check out one last club.

"Come on Bostjan, like Max said in his latest motivational speech, always do one more. ONE MORE!"

"Ahhh, fuck it, okay bro. One more."

We roll in at 4.30 and it's fucking chaos everywhere. A million paper napkins on the floor (the Bulgarian people throw paper napkins in the air at some point in the night, not sure why, but it's amusing), lots of drunk people, some girls still dancing. Thank god the girls at the tables are a bit more relaxed and drunk here, hell, they're even moving and talking a little bit, haha.

I open a few sets here and there, and then I see a group. I'm bored because my buddies are in sets, and so I tap one of the girls on her shoulder.

"Hey!"

She turns around and I can tell she likes me right off the bat. Deep Bambi eyes. I hug her and she's super responsive, stays in the hug and even comes closer, like a little kitten. We don't talk much; in fact, my opener after tap-tap was: "I'm from Slovenia."

A few sentences up and down, she still stays in my hug, I'm thinking about making out. She's ready, I can see and feel that, but her friends are near.

"Do you know where the coat room is?"

She doesn't.

"Ok, I will show you."

Take her to the lobby, sit her down. We exchange a few sentences, the basics. There's passion in the air, I can feel it, and so can she, based on her eyes. I smell her neck and tell her she smells good. She surprises me a little bit and says:

"I want you to kiss me now."

Gotta love girls in Sofia.

I shut the fuck up and kiss her, then pull back away while she wants more. I always try to do this, because if you kiss for too long, the energy just evaporates. It was a pretty good kiss, it only bothered me because I could taste the wine on her lips. But hey, nobody's perfect.

Then we make out more, I touch her face gently, upper breast, shoulders, then again pull away when she wants more. She forgets my name, so I teasingly make her say "I'm sorry, please tell me your name again," in a sexy voice, and then kiss my neck straight after. She plays along and I think it's awesome, plus I just melt when my neck is being kissed.

Oh btw, she's a bit older, around 27, and a bit shorter than me, but very hot. Damn, almost all Eastern European girls are just incredibly sexy. She has a petite body, light brown hair, curls (jackpot) and had what looked like small boobs, which later on turned out to be bigger. Another bonus of Eastern European girls right there, haha.

Well, I screen for logistics then, turns out she lives with her mom.

#Screen Logistics
Get information on where the girl lives, how many friends is she in the club with, and what she is doing the day after. All important factors to consider, when deciding to invite the girl to your/her place or not.

Then I ask if she can make me pancakes.

"You really want to have sex tonight, huh?"

We make out again. By the way, it's getting really hot by now. She tells me she likes me, I tell her I like her too, plus that her neck smells really good. She suggests a hotel, I say that's cool, we can split cost.

Then she asks where my friends are, I say they're just leaving. Money-saving on my mind, I mention I have a place where we could go instead of paying for the hotel. I explain that there's only the living room with a sofa, but that the flatmates will be asleep. She's down for that.

So far so good, we cab it home, but then my host just arrived home at the same time, so he opens the door and introduces himself. Oops, a bit awkward. Then we come up and the second flatmate comes to the kitchen too, it's 5.30am by now.

They open a bottle of wine (omg, why!?), pour some for her and themselves (I take water myself, I'm such a pussy, haha) and start chatting. I chill a bit away from them with my computer and think to myself:

"What the fuck, what the fuck, just go to sleep guys. What the fuck, how can we have sex if you guys are starting the after-party? What the fuck?"

Then one flatmate starts to do the laundry - putting clothes on the drying rack. I go crazy in my mind.

"Seriously bro, you're gonna do laundry at fucking 5am? What the fuck. Ok, be cool man, you've been through worse than that."

I relax a little and then talk to the second flatmate who is smoking, I quietly explain the deal with the girl to him, as if it was not super obvious. He's super cool about it, he understands, says good night after a few minutes, and leaves.

My girl is now helping to do the laundry with the first guy, which is pretty cool actually, I like a girl who doesn't mind helping out. So I just pretend to be on Facebook and chill. To be honest, I can't actually do any work, I'm so horny it's killing me. They're done with the laundry, she goes to the toilet, the 2nd flatmate goes to his room too.

She finally returns and then comes to me, I guess she felt the withdrawal of my attention. She sits close to me, and kisses me gently. I kiss her back, and then our passion starts to burn hot.

We kiss each other, and then start to take each other's clothes off.

She has a really nice body, she's probably an athlete with how fit she is. I couldn't notice that so much before. Nice, slender muscles, tight ass, beautiful breasts. There's also a very sexy tattoo stretching down one of her arms. I kiss the tattoo, she's pulling my hair and massaging my dick. I move away the panties and finger her, god, she was so wet. It always turns me on when a girl is wet for me.

There was no need in taking it slow with her. She was as horny as I was, and she knew what she wanted, and I respect that. That's why I sometimes like older girls more, there's less drama, they know what they want, and don't care as much about the society and whether somebody will judge them or not. Life is short after all.

She feels really good when I penetrate her, she moans softly, and I can still remember a shadowy image of her face covered in curls on that sofa, breathing heavy as I am inside her. She bites my neck and scratches my back pretty hard, it fuels me and I go very deep and very hard. Soon I come on her tits, that was so hot!

She didn't come yet, so I help her out with my hands. It doesn't take too long and then we both collapse on the sofa. I kiss her a bit more, I don't remember if we cuddled or not, but that's probably because we fell asleep in a few mins, we were exhausted and it was probably around 6 or 7am at this point.

One thing I noticed before drifting to sleep, sounds corny but what the hell, is how beautiful she looked when she was asleep. Relaxed expression on her face, calmly breathing, I could see the sides of her hips and a part of her breast, and the rest of her slender figure under the blanket. If I could take a photograph of that, it would be an awesome one. Beautifully erotic.

I fall asleep remembering Max's words from that motivational video:

"Sometimes, it's the last set that you end up pulling.

Always do one more."

Chapter Twenty-Six
TATTOO AND NO COFFEE AFTER SEX

Sofia, November 2015

Days pass, and it's Sunday, the big tattoo day.

I wasn't that nervous. I guess when you only own a suitcase and a backpack and a couple thousand bucks, nothing is that scary anymore. It lasted six hours and after the second hour or so, it started to hurt a lot. But I kind of endured. I distracted my mind with listening to music and audio books. It hurt more in the end, when the pain kind of accumulated.

The guy was an absolute expert, I have to say. He worked fast and precise. And once I saw the masterpiece, I tipped him like I was super rich. It was beautiful, I fell in love with my tattoo, and the love still lasts. In fact, I love it more and more as days pass.

Oh, the motive? It's kind of like a pin-up girl, but an anime version. Actually drawn by my dear sister, who's an awesome manga-style artist. The girl on the tattoo is a really hot. She's a blonde wearing roses in her hair. Dressed in a mini skirt and a very revealing top, with a beautiful face, and big tits. A nice belly too. Why a sexy girl? Well, I figured it will be a great memory of this crazy adventure when I'm old.

There was something bugging me though. I wanted to meet up with the girl I slept with on Tuesday too. She had a lot of tattoos, and obviously I sent her a pic of my newly finished one. She would kind of respond to my texts all week, but on our last full day in Sofia, the tattoo day, she would not meet me.

I would try several times, but she didn't come out. I didn't understand that. She wasn't really busy, she had that Sunday off. We had such a good time, the sex was good too. Or is all just my imagination? Was the sex bad, did I do something wrong? Is it me or is it her? Why would she not want to meet me again?

There was zero logic in that. Ok, I get it, it was just a one night stand. But why would she respond to my texts then. And the texts were super nice too, like almost in a boyfriend-girlfriend kind of way, sending pictures to each other, etc. Maybe it was too much for her, maybe she was afraid of getting close because I was leaving shortly. I don't know. I was confused out of my mind, and a little sad. And very horny.

That was one really fucked up flake.

#Flake
When a girl doesn't respond to your texts or calls, or doesn't show up for a date.

It's not like I had never been flaked on before. In fact, you get flakes ALL the time in game, no matter how good you are. Even Max still gets flakes. But that's not the point. The point is that the flakes suck, and that I don't understand it. A girl clearly enjoys your company, shows willingness to meet up, and then breaks communication. The best and the closest to accurate advice I've gotten about this is:

"Dude, they're girls. They change their mind all the time. One moment she likes you, next one she doesn't. There's no logic."

Now I doubt that it is as simple as that, but I haven't gotten an explanation that would make sense yet. I asked a lot of people and analyzed a lot of personal experiences, nothing gave a good explanation, it's just such an enigma. Is it really just the heat of the moment? But what about the texts then? Blah. I'll just stick to the "they're just girls" argument for now.

During the course of these travels, I would accumulate a SHITLOAD of flakes, which started to add up, you know, in an emotional sense. These flakes would then start to make me feel uneasy and cause pain, and show me the other side of the game, or even of human relationships in general.

Opening up, liking someone, hoping to see them again, and then not ending up doing so.

That sucks.

And that gets you on your way down the rabbit hole before you even realize it...

Chapter Twenty-Seven
FROM GROCERIES
TO BLOW JOB

BJ Report, November 2015

Krakow Inner Circle Facebook Group

So I arrive to Krakow on Monday, the last week of November. At about 8pm I meet with my host (a super cool guy, a Finnish dude living in Krakow). We chat for a bit, I dump my stuff. I still have like two hours off before I have to go work, so my host joins me to the grocery shop.

On the way to the shop we chat, I see some girl looking at me, I smile and wave to her, signal for her to come closer. She comes, we small talk for a bit, I see she's super interested in me. We then talk for five more minutes.

Some teasing and some basic talk, which uni she is going to, how long we're here, etc. Then I tell her we're getting groceries and she should come with (the shop was only one minute away). She hesitates a bit and then joins.

More playful talk, I make her carry my basket, and tell her she's my shopping assistant for the day. Later on I take a funny pic with her and my host, we're having loads of fun. Then I actually do my groceries and let the two of them chat for a while.

After I'm more or less finished I go back to them and again take the leader role. We come out of the shop, I invite her for a drink to our place. She wants to come, but her anti-slut defense kicks in, she says no even though we insist. I ask her to add me on Facebook and off we go.

#Anti-Slut Defense
When a girl is sexually interested with you, but does not want to take things further, because she is concerned with how she might look to others. Example, if she goes home with a guy after just an hour, even though there's an awesome connection or just pure attraction, she would feel guilty and would be considered a "slut" in eyes of others. Also called connected to #Slut-Shaming

Btw, she's 19 years old, curly brown hair. What's up with the curls and me, haha. Her face isn't drop-dead gorgeous, but she has a nice body, and she's fit. She has a contagious smile too. I loved that smile, and she laughs at all my jokes, we had a nice vibe going on. Turns out she's a fresh student, who's new in town. The whole interaction lasted about 60 minutes.

Then I text a little with her the same evening, I send her some selfies, she does the same. I ask what she's doing tomorrow, says she finishes uni at 14.45. Cool, I tell her I'll wake up at 1pm, and that she can join me for coffee.

I text her at 13:45, we meet at the bus stop where I first met her (two minutes from my host's flat). Then I just walk straight to our place with her, not mentioning it at all, just chatting all the time so she's comfortable.

We come up, I introduce her to my host and his flatmate, I take her straight to the room, open the doors to the kitchen, she starts to check out the room and my host chats with her for a bit. I prepare my breakfast and make some coffee.

In about 10 minutes I join her in the room, my flatmates leave for the gym. I eat my breakfast (muesli with yogurt) and talk with her, show her my new tattoo, she touches it gently. I know it's on, based on her touch. Very light, yet caring, and lasts a little longer than would be considered just friendly. It's fucking on.

I finish my muesli (I also didn't have much time because I had to meet Max in an hour or so), slowly lean in and kiss her neck, she loves it. There's a fire in her eyes. We are making out, I take my shirt off first. I know I'm rushing it a little bit, but I really don't have much time, which is sad, because I'd like to take it slower.

Then I try to take off her shirt, she won't let me. Make out again, after some time take off her sweater, she's cool with that, but not the top that was underneath yet. Rinse and repeat, take off the top too. Make her wet, start rubbing her pussy. I try to take off her belt but she stops me and says:

"We have a problem, guess what it is."

"Are you on your period?"

"Nope, try again."

"Are you a virgin?"

"Yes..."

"No worries, we don't have to do anything you won't be comfortable with. I just really want to lick your pussy, imagine how good that would feel."

She started to get crazy wet and horny, her eyes were blazing.

She lets me take the belt off, and I take off her pants too. God, she's so fucking sexy. A perfect ass and long, slim legs. I think she's a bit taller than me. Nice, fit tummy, and really big breasts.

I start to eat her pussy and she's loving it. She has such a sweet pussy too, nicely shaved. I love eating pussy. There's a special feeling we guys get when pleasing a girl, when we see that she's really enjoying it. It makes you feel great about yourself, great about giving an awesome experience to the girl. It also makes you very horny.

With a perfect ass behind the pussy, I realize again, that, oh my god, Eastern Europe is just amazing!

I take off my pants, take out a condom, but she won't let me go any further. I don't mind, I'm having a great time. Plus, my mind is still kind of blown. Keep in mind that all this was happening after about 40 minutes of meeting her. I eat her pussy and finger her at same time, she's loving it. She's shaking all the time, but I'm not sure whether she's coming or just having a really good time.

After my hands get tired, she starts to touch my dick a bit, I put it straight to her mouth and she starts giving me a really nice blow job. She was surprisingly good at sucking my dick, especially for a 19-year old virgin.

While she's doing that I am massaging her amazing tits. I have this mental image of myself sitting on her chest, touching her tits with one hand, massaging her pussy with the other, as she's sucking my dick. That's a really cool image. In the end, she eats the cum. I feel like the king of the world.

We cuddle for a bit, then I need to go so we dress and head out. We agree I'll be meeting her again later on in the week. I really hope I do, because she's cool. The way she's open with her sexuality, yet also clearly establishes boundaries, I really respect that.

No drama, no bullshit, just sharing.

Chapter Twenty-Eight
MEETING THE MOVIE TEAM - HOW REAL ARE YOU?

Tuesday

A special surprise awaited us in Krakow. There was a movie team following us around and filming a lot of the things we did. Long story short, Max agreed to be in a documentary film shot by a guy named Matt, a producer who deals with controversial topics. For example, his previous film was named *"California High"* and discussed the legalization of Marijuana in the State of California.

This time around, he is making a movie about pickup and the game and the pickup industry in general, and obviously he wanted to get his hands on the biggest and best company in the industry - Real Social Dynamics.

And since Max was the only RSD instructor cool with being put into that film, Matt flew to Krakow for a week while we were there to hang out with us, but mostly to shoot us.

Matt's a cool guy. He's tall, in his thirties, and carries a big-ass cool camera around most of the time, at least when I get to see him. Very polite, and has a bright eye contact of someone who is living their dream. There was a girl with him too, only for the week. She was an assistant and she was pretty hot, but let's get to this later.

What surprised me is that Matt not only filmed Max, and the way Max acts, teaches, eats, and basically almost everything there is to film, but he also filmed Vini and I. He filmed how we got the gear ready, he filmed me washing the dishes, he filmed when we were video editing; he tried to capture the whole deal.

He was always super nice to me and even answered some video producing questions I had later on. I couldn't help but like the guy.

So one day, I think early in the week, Matt came with his assistant girl to shoot us in Max's Airbnb. The plan was to also do some short video interviews with all of us.

And here I was again blown away by how many things Max could handle, it was almost superhuman. I still vividly remember a special moment from the kitchen. Matt is arranging the cameras, he's filming Max in 5 minutes.

Max is trying to finish his meal, really clean food he freshly cooked just a few minutes ago. As he's eating, he is responding to Youtube comments. He always responds to every single comment, and he gets thousands.

It might not seem much, but let's take into consideration

the scope of time management like that. Firstly, Max pulled some hot girl the night before and thus didn't get much sleep, straight after Matt's filming, we'd go out to shoot Youtube videos. And then after that would come the editing, hitting the gym and then some more editing. Time management like that, IS a pretty big fucking thing.

Not to mention the biggest chunk of the week was still in front of us, the Free Tour, the Hot Seat, and the Bootcamp.

I wondered if there was any limit to his energy and motivation. It seemed to me absolutely crazy and out of this world. How can twenty-five-year-old be so on top of his life?

What I didn't know then was that there was a price. And the answer would soon start to reveal itself.

Anyway, I agreed to do a short interview for Matt too. He miked me up, and boom, the big-ass camera was pointing straight into my face. His assistant was asking the questions, and told me to keep eye contact with her. That was pretty hard because she was kind of hot.

When I'm looking a hot girl in her eyes, there's usually only one thing in my mind. How it would be to have sex with her. So that made it harder for me to focus on the interview.

I wonder if that was a technique they used. To get the players in their "natural habitat", haha.

I was kind of nervous, and that was new to me. Recently I hadn't been very nervous, even in challenging situations. But I feel my voice shaking a little bit, I hate the big light shining in my face, and I hate the fact that the cute girl was interviewing me. I still see her eyes, and me dabbling between returning her strong eye contact, or focusing on the content of what I was going to say.

All the standard questions about my age and how I found the job came, and what kinds of stuff I do regularly. I talked about the mysterious application, video shooting, meeting Max, the groceries, the preparation of the seminar room, the long editing hours, the travels, and much more. And then she asks about the infield filming. I answer:

"Well, that's pretty cool. I basically take an awesome DSLR camera and follow Max into the night club. There I film him talking to girls, trying to catch good angles and make the image perfect. I'm becoming pretty good at it too, I know how to use all the manual functions now, I know about the light, etc."

And for some reason, I think that isn't enough and I continue:

"Also, I don't think that's illegal at all. It's kind of a grey zone. It's legal to film people in public spaces, and clubs are considered such places. Plus, I only film Max, and don't focus on the girls, because what he does matters to our viewers. We censor all of the girls' identities anyway."

At that point I notice Max looking from the computer screen towards me. I don't even know how I noticed that, but I guess you get a sort of a sixth sense for the people you know really well. So I kinda know there was something off about that question. But it's too late now, the words have already left my mouth.

After the session ended, Matt leaves and we head to meet the students. On the way, Max tells me some things:

"Well, fuck. You gave them all they wanted, bro. I mean, I don't blame you, they ask sneaky questions, but I was hoping something like this wouldn't come out. They can twist it around hardcore. Take a sentence out of a context, and you're in for some trouble."

Vini, who also did the interview, but seemingly better, added:

"Dude, that's how they work. They act all nice and helpful, and then stab you in the back in the end. It's a part of the job. They create crazy rapport by becoming friends with you, asking you all this personal questions and vibing with you. And then you provide all the info he needs. You just got fucked bro. And not only you, Max too.

Now I'm not saying Matt will do this, let's wait and see. But it's just that I know how the media can distort the real picture. It's very simple to present the argument from only one side. And well, you being the interviewed person, well, you don't get to pick which side that is."

Damn, I could see some truth in that, and Matt shone in a brand new light in my eyes. I realized I pretty much fucked up on the interview. Fuck. But at least Max took it well. He didn't blame me or anything, he just told me what was up, I appreciated that.

I also met Matt later on in Miami, where he was filming us again. He still seemed like a super cool dude and I can't find anything going against him. I even pushed him into a set with some hot girl on our last night out, when he was just hanging out with us.

"This is Matt, he's a famous movie director."

The girl was all over him in a second. He could have fucked her easily, but was a bit too much of a chode for that. Or maybe he just didn't like her. I don't know to be honest.

I guess I'll just have to wait for the movie to come out, to see what happened with my interview.

Oh, I said I wanted to talk about the assistant girl too, huh? Well, she was Polish, in some film school, and that's how she applied for Matt's position. These film guys have a wide network all over the world.

Anyhow, she was not traditionally super hot, but she had a different kind of "hotness" to her. Average size, nice body, long, straight brown hair. Yet, she was ambitious, and there was a certain gleam in her eyes. That gleam gave her an aura of incredible sexuality, I can imagine sex with her would be really good.

In addition, she was young, and I guess it turned her on being around pickup dudes. I mean, I don't want to brag, but Team RSD Max was a group of 3 young, cool dudes who were in good shape and had their shit together, plus could hold their ground talking to any girl. Not many guys of similar age can claim that.

So yeah, even through just eye contact, she seemed super down. One day while we were filming day game, she even teasingly asked:

"Bostjan, I've seen Vini do some approaches, why don't you do some, to show me how it's done?"

And similar shit like that. A bit of playful teasing and testing, and it was cool, I love that. We also had some conversations with pretty heavy eye contact and energy back at Max's Airbnb. My plan was to invite her for a drink on Sunday evening.

However, Max and Vini noticed she's down too, and Max prepared a naughty plan of how we could invite her over and potentially have group sex with her if she was down. I liked the idea. However, Sunday evening came and went, and Max seemed to forget all about it.

God dammit, I really wanted to try it out with this girl, I kinda never forgave him this one. I mean, it's not a big deal, but I did kinda like that girl, might have been an amazing romance. And I bet she wanted to fuck a player too.

Later on, I thought about my interview for the pickup movie on many more occasions. My opinion is still kind of the same. I pretty much honestly fucked up, I acted in good fashion, but they can really distort that if they want to.

However, call me naive, and maybe I'll hit myself on the head after re-reading this in the future, but I still kind of trust Matt, and think the movie is gonna turn out all right.

Chapter Twenty-Nine
KRAKOW GIRLS AND ON HAVING CANCER

Wednesday

I love Krakow, man, my favorite city of the whole tour. There are a lot of things to love about Krakow. It's amazingly cheap. It's very beautiful with a super cool medieval inner city. You can go out pimping every day of the week, even Sunday. And the best thing, the girls there are hot. And not just hot, they are very feminine as well. So let me tell you about Krakow girls.

Krakow girls are amazing. Not as hot as girls in Sweden for example, but they come very close. However, there is this awesome feminine energy around them. It's like they love being girly. They want to take care of a man. Sounds super stereotypical, but this type of girl will love to cook for you, clean up your place and massage you (and give an awesome blowjob) once you come home from work.

Now obviously, this is just my generalization. I'm not saying all girls in Krakow are like that, and that no girl anywhere else possess these qualities. However, I noticed more of that in Krakow and Eastern Europe in general, and I really like it, it sat well with me.

It's a perfect counterbalance to the masculine energy, the one that is always working and achieving, dominating. If it never takes time off, it can become manic and destructive. If you have ever read '*The Way of The Superior Man,*' or any other literature concerning male and female energies, you will know what I am talking about.

Anyway, I was meeting the BJ girl again on Wednesday.

We didn't have sex, but it was still a very hot time.

She just loved my dick, and I don't mean it in a demeaning way. Some girls, they just love the D. They love playing with it, they love sucking it, they love it when it's inside of them. Other girls kind of endure the D, you know, they give blowjobs and hand jobs, but mostly because they know guys really like it, or because they want to be nice for their boyfriend. But they don't really enjoy it.

Well, not her.

By the way, it was not "just" about sexual pleasure. This time we properly hung out, it was awesome. We kissed a lot, we cuddled in the bed, we talked. We talked about my travels, what I want to do in life, where she is now, how it feels in a new city for her as a student. What the future holds for both of us.

I love discovering the inner world of another person. It's

so rich, beautiful, and completely unique for each and every one of us. Sometimes, if you just shut up and listen, you can learn so much, and experience so much wonder.

At some point she said she loved my life force.

I find it a bit unusual, but thank her for it. She then continues and tells me how she actually overcame cancer not so long ago. She shows me the tits I love so much and tells me that one of them is actually fake, as they had to cut her own away. I see a little scar just under her boob.

Wow, it seems this 19-year old girl has already been through a lot in her life. I guess that's why she was not that concerned with the society's expectations and was cool with hooking up with a cool guy relatively fast.

If today was your last day, and you had met a cool guy or a girl, and you would both be really attracted to each other, would you fuck them or not? She liked me, I liked her, so why not spend some time together? Hypothetical situations like this give some perspective.

After she told me that, I hugged her, and I kissed her passionately. And I didn't feel sorry for her one bit, she was such an amazing, lively, sexy girl. And I told her that. She started to glow.

We talked more after that, it opened up a new world. I asked her if she knows the beautiful story of *The Alchemist*, by Paulo Coelho. She didn't and I shorty explained what it was.

And then, because I actually had the book with me, a gift from a friend of mine from the previous city, I gave it to her. I told her to read it, and then pass it on to another person who would know how to appreciate it.

I don't know how the book is doing now, but I think it's still with her. Ah well.

The week in Krakow was very busy. Not only did we have a full week of programs with a the Hot Seat, the Free Tour, and the Bootcamp. We also had the film crew following us. I was also gaming like crazy, I met a lot of girls in that week.

Another really awesome thing happened in Krakow. You know how we had a few crazy nights with the guys? The pure bromanship with Max and Vini? Well, I'd say my favorite one was the Oslo night with the boys, super fun, plus I pulled too.

The second one was the Zurich Pants Down Craze.

But Krakow, in Krakow I spent the best night with my man Vini. This night bonded the two us forever.

"Gaaaaaay!"

Chapter Thirty
BRO BONDING AND SINK EJACULATION

Thursday, 3am, After The Bootcamp

I was tired, yet excited from all the hot girls in the club. Max didn't pull this night, too bad, because if he did, it would have been a hat trick – he pulled 2 nights in a row in the days before. I decide I'm not ready for the bed yet, and will pimp it with Vini for a bit more.

I walk through the club. It's more empty than before, a lot less hotties, dammit. I see a girl on the dance floor, and motion to her with finger: *"you're a bad girl"* (similar to how parents show the motion to small children). She's like *"what!?"* with a smile on her face. I persist with non-verbals for a minute, then I come close and whisper in her ear:

"You're a bad girl!"

Bostjan Belingar

And she loves it.

I don't say anything else, but just come close and start to grind with her, it's that part of the night already, you can almost do anything you want. She and I are both loving it. After about ten minutes I am too physical, being very touchy and sexual, and not giving her any space to chase me. The energy drops.

I realize that, stop what I'm doing, and up my verbal game. Crack a few jokes, tease her a bit. She loves me again. I try to reinitiate the dance because I love dancing dirty with a girl. It was too late though, I didn't calibrate fast enough. The energy isn't fully there anymore and I'm trying a bit too hard. She can feel that too, so she drifts away.

Vini had already left for some street game by now. I wander around and I open a few more sets, but nothing really hooks. The club is getting super empty, super fast. Ah, well. I guess it's a jerk off night again. You'd be surprised at how many of those you have as a dating coach's assistant, haha.

I open a girl at the bar waiting for her drink, and funny enough, she hooks. My opener is weird, and I say some stupid shit on how to eat avocado, it's not even funny, but I just hang around and not care too much anyway. I'm a dude who has fun and an "IDGAF (I Don't Give A Fuck)" attitude. She tests me a little bit: *"Where are your friends?"* *"Why are you talking to me?"* but nothing crazy. She wants to go back to her friend.

I ask her if she will dance (I was tired, and I wouldn't go with her if she did want to dance), and she said no.

"Ok, introduce me to your friends then."

And I just start to lead her in the direction where I supposed her friends were.

"Uhm, ok..."

I get introduced to her friend who loves me instantly. I got a good social position because her friend brought me and introduced me. It's always easier when you are introduced. I also crack a few jokes:

"Thought your friend was 19, she looks so cute..."

I vibe with both, they ask again where my friends are. I said one's coming and start showing them pictures and videos of Vini from my phone, because I dunno what to talk about next, I am just really tired. I even show them a pic of topless Vini, doing a backspin from the night before.

I text Vini at this point:

"Dude, I need a wing, two-set, flatmates, they are down and kinda cute, come help."

Being an amazing bro and wing, he comes at just the right moment, just as the girls are about to leave. I give him the petite girl because I know he likes skinnier women. I take mine, who is also cute, but not as petite. And then the good times start.

We walk hand in hand through the rain with them, the small girl loves Vini. We find some late night food & drink place in about five minutes, it's roughly 4am. The place is awesome. It's in the old city centre, they sell beer for 1€

and awesome burgers with fries for 2€. I don't really care about beer, but I mean, how cheap is that? I think I had at least five burgers in that place during the course of the week.

We find a table, the girls get us some shots. Fuck, neither of us drinks.

"Fuck it bro, it's Krakow, and the last beer we had was a month ago."

We sit at the table, my girl almost didn't want to sit on the bench next to me, she wanted a chair, I tease her a bit and take a step back:

"Relax, I won't touch you or anything like that, just come closer."

So yeah, we have the shots, and then in the course of an hour or so two more rounds come - I buy one, and then the girls get the next.

Vini is smart and avoids getting drunk. When the round comes, he swallows and then spits out the content of the shot into a glass of water without anyone noticing. The girls don't notice because he's such a gangster and I only knew because he texted it to me. I drank all my shots because I didn't figure out a solution as he did, so I got drunk. Pretty stupid of me, but kind of fun too.

And in case you were wondering, why most players don't like to drink? Well, there's a lot of reasons. You save money. You save health. You are productive the next day, you remember who you talked to through the night, etc. There's all these positives to not drinking. However, it's a bit socially odd, people give you a funny look when you're sober in a club and drink water.

Anyway, besides me getting drunk, we both focus on our girls. I build a super strong connection with mine, she doesn't like the physicality, so I focus on emotions, we really connect with books, she tells me what she reads, I ask how it makes her feel, etc. I mention crying when I re-read the Alchemist. Shit just like that, and we both get super open. She's a bit resistant to opening up at first, but I tell her why I believe it's good:

"Being open and vulnerable is good and brave. It helps create a stronger connection with people. This is how you can quickly find out if the people care about the real you, not just some fake persona you carry around..."

She slowly starts to open up, I guess she agreed. I love the vibe. I wasn't able to even make out or kiss her neck, but I loved those moments. Like seriously, it sounds super gay, but just touching her face and feeling her tremble under my palms and things like that felt really good, the whole masculine-feminine vibe. I enjoyed every second of it.

Anyway, I'm getting drunk, and so are the girls. Vini is cheating, though, that Brazilian bastard. We need to pull fast, it's getting late, close to 5am, and we don't want the girls to drink too much, that's never good. Vini has an awesome idea on how to pull, texts me the details, and gets a naughty grin on his face. He says:

"Fuck, my phone died, I have my home address in it, I need to charge it."

The helpful girls don't follow Vini's plan, which was to go home to their place to charge the phone. Instead, one of them goes and borrows a charger at the bar and brings it to us. So much for a pull excuse, well done, Vini, haha.

And Vini was so damn proud about his idea too, I almost die laughing when one of the girls brought the charger back from the bar. Dammit. It was really funny though, I think I almost fell off the bench.

Then I build more connection with my girl, and talk about how she will show me her books that she has at home. She even pinky promised on that. Totally seeded the pull there. Then we go out to buy a bottle of Zyubrowka (a type of vodka) and some Snickers bars, because I love that shit, and then head straight for the taxi.

My girl gives some shit when the taxi rolls in:

"Where are we going, we can't go to our place, let's go back to the bar and have another drink..."

Again, classic anti-slut thoughts in their heads. They clearly liked us, we were having an awesome time, but if they just came with us with zero excuses, they would be considered easy.

"It's ok baby, just for half an hour, it's warm, we'll just be drinking and hanging out, no pressure."

We enter the cab without looking back.

They follow, sweet!

Vini and I have the biggest grins ever, it's going amazing. I mean, keep in mind, pulling doesn't always happen. From reading all these stories it might sound like we pull every night. Well, no. There are a lot of nights when you just go home and sleep. Or jerk off and sleep. So this was already one of the good nights.

When we come to their place, we realize something important. They are roommates, not flatmates. This makes it a bit more complicated. Fuck.

Vini's girl undresses so he also does same and they go under the covers, making out and shit. I chill with my girl on the bed, listening to Youtube. Slightly awkward listening to the two in the bed, but music helps. More deep talks and sad music (James Blunt) connect us further. I sit behind her, hold/embrace her, she lets me do that, and now it feels good.

We are just hugging there on the bed. We talk about our deepest wishes, she wants to visit Alaska, just like in the movie *"Into The Wild."* I encourage her and tell her I really think she should go, before she forgets the dream or becomes too old. I then slowly and gently kiss her neck. It's kinda like taming a cat, you have to be super careful, because if you push too far or too fast it runs away.

Oh btw, it's fucking 6.30am. I'm tired and losing my patience, but I'm becoming a seasoned veteran so I don't show it. Rushing never helps. Then I massaged her, first through her clothes, then removed her top and bra, she's wearing only pants now. Massage feels good for her and it's making me really horny. Her naked back and a nicely shaped butt under me, I can feel my dick getting harder. I say:

"C'mon let's lie down for a bit and cuddle."

We lie down, but we still don't kiss. I kissed most of her body by now, I massaged her ass and her pussy, but didn't get to make out with her. However, now she finally starts to get into it. Her hips start moving, she touches my dick through the pants.

I gently pull her into the first kiss, and then she REALLY gets into it. Some hardcore passionate making out, groping, biting, and scratching follow. Then I lose most of my clothes, finger her, make out with her more, and lick her titties. Super nice titties actually, again all hail Krakow girls.

I was also telling her how I want to fuck her first gently and then really hard, dirty-talking like a pro. We are both in our underwear, and just when we'd finally get to the action, her alarm rings.

It's 7.30 am. She needs be at some important uni discussion at 9.

Fuck!

I finger her super hard, she's super horny and wet, I'm hoping we can have a quickie, but she says:

"I'm sorry, I'd like to have sex with you, but I really need to go."

Up until now, I was super on point, non-needy, not try-hard. Basically, an awesome player, one who could turn the girl on properly, and give her what she wants, disregarding all the testing and other BS.

But when she stood up and left for the bathroom, I lost it.

I was super horny, like SUPER HORNY. Not just horny. I MEAN SUPER DUPER HORNY! I'd probably fuck a hole in the wall at that point, I don't know if you can relate to this, but that was really intense. I guess my meditation teachers wouldn't be proud of my "attachments" to passion at that point.

Anyway, I follow her to the bathroom, and ask her to jerk me off quickly. She doesn't want to do that, as she is brushing her teeth.

I take out my dick, stand behind her, put my hand down her top, start to squeeze her boobs, and tell her to make out with me as I am masturbating. She kisses me back passionately and willingly. I guess it was turning her on too – she made a guy so horny that he was masturbating right next to her.

Just imagine this scene, a sleep deprived girl with messed up make up standing in her bathroom, in front of the mirror. A toothbrush in her hand. Behind her a guy stands just in his underwear. They are kissing, and the guy is masturbating with one hand, and grabbing the girl's breasts with the other. As I'm about to come she says:

You better not come on my clothes, I don't have the time to change them!"

So I did what I could, I came in their sink.

After that my non-neediness is back. I joke around while she gets ready, we take the tram together, and let the other two sleep. We are just chatting and teasing each other, almost girlfriend-boyfriend style. On the tram, we promise we will meet later that day, hopefully in the evening. I get some croissants on the way and give her one. We take a selfie together and say bye-bye.

I step out of the tram at 9am, feeling like a BOSS. Jerking off in her sink felt as good as if we would have gone all the way. You see, I slowly started to grasp it was not all about the sex. Super amazing connection, being horny, dirty talking, spending a night with a cute chick and my best buddy. These epic stories will remain in my memory forever, having sex or not. And epic stories deserve a boss walk.

I actually see girls staring at me because my grin is so big. It's almost as if they can sense it. This guy had some sexy time this night. But even funnier is, I don't give a fuck. I just spread my grin further and walk. Oh, I also have a big ass Snickers in my hands, because it just felt right.

And then just because I can, I run after some hottie, a real stunner, who checked me out too. I open her easily, walk with her, and number-close her. The number did kinda flake in the end, but yeah my boss walk was amazing.

I am super grateful for this amazing night, loved the goofing around with my boy almost more than the girl (gaaaaaay), built a super strong connection with a cute girl, enjoyed her opening up to me like a flower, shared masculine and feminine energy, and infamously ejaculated in a sink.

That's a story worth telling your grandchildren to.

Well, maybe not.

Chapter Thirty-One
FIRST BREAKDOWN

Saturday

Saturday was a grim day. On most Saturdays, Vini and I would wake up super early, around 9am with only a couple of hours' sleep, since we were doing the usual Bootcamp routine on Friday night. We dragged our asses to the seminar room in some random hotel, set everything up, and then chilled for a bit.

Even the room itself had a grim vibe to it. It was not very big, and weirdly lengthy. The windows were small, and the projector was really shitty. The weather outside was rainy and foggy and it was starting to get cold.

After we initially set up everything, I did some video editing and regular stuff while Max talked on for hours during the Hot Seat. I was feeling especially tired that day and some other stuff bugged me too. For example, the BJ-giving virgin girl from earlier this week kinda flaked. I really wanted to see her before I left, I wanted some cuddling and warmth, in weather like this it's easy to feel blue.

I was also thinking about when to shoot my own weekly video. On top of all the work I had to do for Max, I was shooting one video a week for my personal Youtube channel: "*BossLifeHacks*." And the tiredness was real, I had had a couple of sleep-deprived nights this week already.

I didn't have my usual smile on that Saturday. Usually, there's a big grin on my face most of the time. Even when bad stuff happens, I laugh about it, or make stupid jokes. But when the going gets really tough, I lose my smile.

Around 5pm, when I was sitting at the entrance desk and video editing, something clicks inside of me. I can't remember what the trigger was, but I suddenly felt as if I was suffocating. I desperately needed air. I ask Vini to cover me at the door (we would monitor people going in and out) and I went outside.

As I am walking through the foggy and darkening city, thoughts are rushing in. What the fuck am I doing here? I am in a strange alien city, I don't know anyone here, I'm burning my money, and it's going down fast. I haven't even gotten laid in a while. It's pretty dark stuff. I work too much, and I'm just so tired.

I find a bench in the park and sit on it. It's slightly drizzling now, but I don't really pay any heed to it. More thoughts come rushing in. I think about my friends back in Slovenia and London, and about my breakdance crew. I think about my family. I think about how I wanted to spend this autumn and winter in sunny and warm Thailand, how I actually hate cold and dark winters. It's been ages since I did some breakdancing too. I realize the lifestyle I am living right now has two sides to it.

It's not just flashy girl-chasing and traveling. It's hard fucking work. Changing country every week. Packing up all your shit into a fucking bag and heading to the next city, the next couch. Finding yourself in a different city where you know nothing and no one. Finding the next girl who you will give your all to, and then who you won't get to see a second time. And if the emotional trauma alone is not enough, add in a healthy 80-hour work week as well.

Oh, and don't forget the messed up circadian rhythms too: going to bed at 4am and waking up around 12pm, and that's when you're lucky. This is far from amazing for your body. I felt like I was trapped. Like I was working non-stop, like the night is really getting dark, and there's no light at the end of the tunnel.

All these thoughts come rushing in and it makes me feel very sad. It was not one thing that was bothering me in particular, but I guess all the things kinda accumulated in the melting pot. And I was "too busy" to monitor or release that in a controlled way, so I did what I could, I started crying. I think the thought of home brought the first tears, and then a lot of them followed.

To be honest, I think I cry quite regularly in life, about once a month probably. On the tour that increased slightly, to about two or three times a month for sure, although not always for sadness. And to brag a little, I have this nice way of crying.
I don't sob like crazy or anything like that. I am very peaceful, I imagine I portray a deeply sad expression and I always try to let the tears just flow. But only when I'm alone. I only let people very close to me see me cry.

So I sit there in some little park in the middle of the Krakow old town, on some unnamed bench and cried. I felt the rain on my skin, I felt the cold, but my tears were warm. And it feels good. And after 20 minutes or so, I feel better. As if the pressure was somewhat released. I felt lighter, as if some of the weight dropped off of my chest. After that, the thoughts become less dark. I could see the sky slowly turning brighter.

Being in the park helped as well. There have been a few turning points in my life, times of deep sadness, and nature has always helped at those times. We call it "Mother Nature" for a reason, it's like a container that can take anything. The amount of shit you carry inside of you is nothing for the mighty container of Mother Nature. At least that's how I see it.

After some time, I stand up, grab my bag, and leave. On the way back, I pass a street musician playing on accordion. It was a sad song, a familiar tune, but I could not connect it to a song I knew. I stop off at a store. I buy a large portion of the most unhealthy-looking chocolate cake I can find - I needed some comfort food at the time and I didn't care whether it was healthy or not.

I came back to the Hot Seat location. I hope the tears dried and won't be noticed anymore. A funny and nonsensical thought crossed my mind:

"Here's a warm welcome to Bostjan, the pimp with awesome game, the assistant of RSD Max himself.

He just returned from his crying session."

Anyway, I sat down, took my cake, opened a yogurt, and started eating. I felt better. I remember having a chat with a French guy, who I met a few weeks ago at the London Hot Seat. He was a really happy guy and some of his positivity and enthusiasm passed on to me. His smile was contagious, and I felt a slight smile creeping up on my lips too. Not for long, but it was there.

I had taken a hit, but I was back up.

I was always pretty good at taking hits, literally and metaphorically. I could take a beating when I was doing martial arts and boxing for several years. I was kind of like Rocky. I was always pretty strong and fast, but not the fastest, not the strongest. But I could endure a lot of pain, I didn't mind it that much. Furthermore, sometimes that would even fuel me and made me perform better, fight better.

And I could take an emotional beating too. I learned how to handle that back when I used to work in psychotherapy with aggressive kids. The amount of negative emotions - anger, guilt, void, frustration, you receive from these kids is overwhelming. Everybody breaks there, you cannot possibly withstand that. So the only solution is to break as soon as possible, so you can get your shit together, and come back.

And this was a valuable skill I had.

Because my crying in the park that day in Krakow was just a prelude. As Team RSD Max embarked from Eastern Europe to the Nordic countries and as the season turned from late-autumn to winter, there was some very dark shit in store for all of us.

At that point, I realized I was falling into the rabbit hole...

Glossary

The Game
A book by Neill Strauss, and a concept of the male-female seduction process, the techniques and explanations. You can have game, or a lack of it. You can do game, you can game with others, you can game girls, or be gamed, or you can be a student of the game.

Pimping
Pimping (it) – a slang term which means going out and talking to women which you didn't know before. Another term for it is "cold approach pickup". Usually used by guys in the seduction community.

Wingman
Your friend who helps you get the girl. Either by just hanging out with you and thus putting you in an awesome mood, or by actually talking to the girl's friends etc, allowing you to focus on the girl.

Open
The act of starting the interaction with an unknown person. Either verbal by saying "Hi", or something else, or nonverbal, for example by eye-contact, gestures or touch.

Bambi Eyes
When a girl's pupils are very dilated, looking straight into your eyes, almost without blinking. You can kind of feel the energy and the "chemistry" as some people would say.

Set
A group of people around the girl you want to talk to. It can be only 2 people, the girl and a friend, or it can be a big group.

Inner Circle
A dedicated Facebook group where players meet and discuss different topics. It's a place to find new wingmen, it's a place to ask questions, a place to share ideas and resources. Amazing places, that help the community grow.

Player
A guy (or a girl) who games.

Approach
Same as # Open.

Hook
Hook is a term for a point where a girl is more inclined to stay and talk to you than to leave. She's comfortable being around you for the time, and from there on you can build up on your interaction.

Cocky-Funny
A slang term coined by David D, suggesting a guy be a combination of a funny guy and a dick when he talks to a girl to make her attracted to him. A cocky-funny guy.

Game Fanboy
A dude who watches way too many game videos and who's read way too many books on the topic. Someone who thinks that RSD instructors are basically Gods and eat pussy for breakfast. I used to be one.

Pulling
Going home or to another private location with the girl, from the venue your are at currently.

Butt Hurt
A slang term for a guy who's acting like a little bitch. A girl

doesn't do as he likes, he starts making up drama and blaming her etc. Being Butt Hurt is never good, but happens to the best of us. Another word would be #Needy, as in "needing" the girl to do or not do something, and being emotionally dependent on that.

#Takeaway

When a girl doesn't do what you want her to, you withdraw most of, or all of your attention. Complete emotional withdrawal, it hurts more than fists. And that's why it works. It's highly manipulative, so special care needs to be taken when using this. Or better, don't use it at all.

#Chode

Is a guy who is afraid of being a guy. He's afraid to show that he likes a girl, he thinks liking sex is bad, he feels bad about expressing what he really feels and wants. A lot of this is to blame on the whole society's instruction of what a cool guy should be but not all of it. We also call chode pretty much any guy who does not know about the game.

#Close

Close is an end-point stage in interaction between a guy and a girl. There's different closes, for example the number-close, or #close, kiss-close. There's the old school slang term f-close, which means a fuck-close. You also have a Facebook-close or basically any other close you can think of.

#In/Out Of State

When you're in state, you feel amazing. You had it in your life before too, it can happen in sports, your job, at a game. It's when everything seems to click, it's when you open girls and they all hook. It's when you get make outs just like that. It's when you have zero fear and feel invincible. How to get that? Usually it's a process of talking to so many girls that you don't care anymore. You let go of your fears and restrictions and just become truly *genuine and in the moment. But there's random factors too. It's quite hard to explain.*

#Isolate
When you move a girl to the bar or some other area of the club where you two can have a conversation. For example, if she's around her friends, it's a lot less likely she'll be okay with you two kissing, because all the friends might judge her. If you guys are alone, that's not an issue.

#Seed the Pull
When you start making future plans for the night with the girl. Either mentioning the two of you might get some food later on, or check out a movie, or get a drink, or have a walk. Basically, anything that signals you want to spend more time with her. So when the clubs closes, or when you make a move, she kinda knows, she's not surprised.

#Self-Amusement
A principle in game. You should never be dependent on how you feel internally on external stimuli, meaning your friends, alcohol, music, or some girl's approval. You should find this in yourself. To make it more practical, an example is you talking about Borat jokes in the club, even though the other speaker might not consider them funny. But you do, and that's what matters. If they don't like that, they are free to leave, and you can find someone who will enjoy jokes like that.

#Screen Logistics
Get information on where the girl lives, how many friends is she in the club with, and what she is doing the day after. All important factors to consider, when deciding to invite the girl to your/ her place or not.

#Flake

When a girl doesn't respond to your texts or calls, or doesn't show up at a date.

#Anti-Slut Defense
When a girl is sexually interested with you, but does not want to take things further, because she is concerned with how she might look to others. Example, if she just goes home with a guy after an hour, even though there's awesome connection or just pure attraction, she would feel guilty and considered a "slut" in eyes of others. Also called connected to #Slut-Shaming

Acknowledgements

This is, quite egoistically, one of my favorite parts of the book. I like being grateful, and there are a lot of people to be grateful to in the process of putting out this book.

First of all, to the heroes of the book, Max and Vini, for accepting me on the road with them for so long, and for keeping me company on the biggest adventure of my life (so far). Without them, not one of these words on the page would have come to be.

To all the amazing women I've meet on the travels in Vienna, Oslo, Berlin, Sofia, Bucharest, Krakow, London, Helsinki, Tallinn. I will not forget you ladies, our times together, and my lessons. I hope I get to see some of you again.

To all the early readers of this book. It would never ever become this good without you, thank you!

To all the hosts that offered me their couch, room, bed, or floor. I am deeply grateful. When I have enough money to rent a nice apartment for myself, I will always keep an extra room, and invite people from all over the world to crash there for free. I promise.

To my bros, Ward and Benjamin, that have my back when I need it. And to Ward, additionally, for making me apply for the job in the first place.

To my family, for supporting what I do.

To Alex, for showing me what love is.

To Fernando from ClickDo, to push me into becoming a personal brand, and for financial support along the way. I would not have made it without you.

To my brother Simon, for the help and support in the whole process. And even more importantly, to teach my one of the most important truths ever - that Google knows everything.

To my stupid boss, who let me quit my job as a therapeutic youth worker a few months prior to the tour. I'd never experience this bitter sweet adventure without her being so dumb.

To the community. For the years of support in the form of random comments, likes, field reports and advice. Both on and off-line. For motivation to persist and improve. I wouldn't have made it solo.

Author Bio

Bostjan has always liked reading. As a 9 year old child he read Lord of the Rings three times, both in Slovenian and English. He was familiar with most of the books on the shelf at the local library.

However, as testosterone took its course, the avid reader started to focus much more of his attention on women and sports than reading. So instead of reading, he'd prefer to breakdance, go out and drink, and think about how cool it would be to actually get laid.

In the early adult years, he started to move around the world a lot. That included an exchange year in Lithuania, a year of working with aggressive kids in London, and then finally traveling the world with an elite dating coach.

The love of reading somehow emerged back to the surface in the form of writing, and the result is the book you have in front of you right now.

If you have any questions or would like to say hello, don't hesitate to contact him via email at bostjan.belingar@gmail.com, or engage him on his social media or blog.

Further Resources

If you're inspired and interested after reading about these adventures, here's a few ideas on what to do next:

1) Follow Bostjan on www.bosslifehacks.com. There's a lot of advice, stories, and epiphanies touching on various subjects. It's a sort of playground where everything is allowed. You will also find **Bosslifehacks** on Youtube.

Make sure to put in your email address/subscribe there - I'll update you when part 2 comes out, and shoot you a value-giving email once or twice a month. No spamming, I promise.

2) Make me a favor:

If you liked this book, please drop a review on Amazon. This is one of the main factors that influences people's buying decisions. So if you take a minute to drop a review (it can be super short), I will be eternally grateful. Plus you increase your karma +5.

3) If you're interested in seduction, game, and players, there's a lot you can do. If you want to learn the techniques yourself, check out an ultimate course called The Natural on basically everything you need to know from my good friend and the hero of this book, RSD Max.

In fact, because you bought this book, you're even entitled to 10% off the price of the product. Just visit www.becomingthenatural.com and enter this coupon code for discount: ELITETRAVEL.

Sample Chapter from Part 2:

50) I Run My First Bootcamp

London, January 2016

Damn. That blonde was super hot. A Swedish girl, 20 years old, with super tight body. She was slightly drunk, out on a Thursday evening on her last night in London. No shit, she was down to have sex that night.

However, the student always has the priority. And then instead of having sex with this super hot blonde, I watched how the student "ruined" the set. And then I masturbated at home. Damn, I know how Max feels at times now.

It all began a few hours ago, when I met my two students at the local casino on Leicester Square. It's a good meeting (or date) spot, nice and comfy, open all night, clean toilets. Hell, you even get free drinks in most casinos.

It was my first time running a Bootcamp. Unofficially, of course. I also didn't charge for it. One student was Ward, a good friend of mine, who actually persuaded me to become an assistant in the first place, so I wanted to give him something in return. And the other was the guy who had given me his room in London for the fourteen days.

The last part of the crew was Pete, a guy who I knew from my earlier pimping days in London. He had sick game, pulled both times when I went out with him, and he had coached at Vegas Immersion, another RSD program, for some time. I have a lot of respect for this guy.

So the two guys roll in, me and Pete are already waiting. I do the bro handshake for my friend Ward and introduce myself to Rish. They were both normal, late 20s, decent sense of fashion, and not socially super awkward. Cool, no hard-case newbies.

We head straight to the club, since it's already close to 11pm. I don't want to risk us not getting in. We get in easily, helped by my strict requests to be smartly dressed. I sit them down at the table and give them an outline of the weekend. Basically, more or less all the stuff I learned from Max:

"Hey guys, by now you know me, I'm Bostjan, and I've been gaming for about 6 years now. The last 3 months, I was traveling around the world with RSD Max, THE fastest-growing game coach right now. We've had Bootcamps and the Hot Seat almost every single weekend for the past 3 months. Trust me when I say this, I've seen it all.

All the sticking points, all the excuses, all the fixes. Trust me, if you do what I say, you will progress in the game. My role here is to push you out of your comfort zone, to give you feedback, and to inspire you, so you'll see me in action too.

Now, you have to know some things too. This is not a Thailand Sex tour, the goal here is not "just" to get laid. Okay, if it happens, cool. But the goal is to teach you how to be self-sufficient. In three days I wont be here to push you anymore, so you better learn how to do this for yourself..."

After the briefing, we went straight to action. I point some girls out to the guys and they go and open them.

Rish is too aggressive, he doesn't have a lot of fear, but struggles to stay in set with the girl for long. Also, he has massive filters and uses a lot of bullshit ideas he had previously "learned" from some other pickup and dating companies. Things like scripted lines, routines, etc. Things that might work initially, but once you want to actually connect and share with the girl, it backfires.

Ward is a bit more experienced, but also more stifled. He tries too hard to "just make the girl like him." He also gets easily discouraged after a rejection and takes it very personally. He's a super cool and funny guy, he's smart, makes a lot of money, but there's a deep sense of "not being enough" in him. Like so many other guys, even me, in the field.

So towards the end of the first night we end up on the same table. Two chicks, Rish, me, and Ward. Pete is in set with the third girl of our two-girl set somewhere else. Ward is doing phenomenally, and after a bit of my help via texting, he moves closer to his girl, vibes, and later on makes out with her.

Rish is trying to get the blonde attracted. However, it's backfiring as it usually does when you try too hard. And again, as it usually happens, she instead focuses on the guy who didn't give a shit: in this case, me.

So while she's asking me questions and being touchy feely with me, Rish is trying desperately to get her attention back. Because I know he likes her, I don't really interact with her, which in turn makes her even more attracted. Weird logic, but some girls actually think like this:

"Why doesn't that guy give a shit about me, I'm super hot... I'll

MAKE him notice me..."

And it was my mistake to be honest; she was hot, I did want her, and she clearly wanted me. However, I didn't want to be a dick to Rish. The guy gave me his own room for two weeks, and that's worth a lot of money if you are living in London. Also, it was the first time we've met.

Fuck my life, I had no idea of what to do...

CPSIA information can be obtained
at www.ICGtesting.com
Printed in the USA
LVHW02s2201201217
560369LV00024B/4105/P